THE

POETICAL WORKS

OF

ROBERT SOUTHEY.

IN TEN VOLUMES.

VOLUME VII.

BOSTON:
LITTLE, BROWN AND COMPANY.
NEW YORK: PHINNEY, BLAKEMAN AND MASON.
CINCINNATI: RICKEY, MALLORY AND CO.
M.DCCC.LX.

BOSTON:
STEREOTYPED BY JOHN WILSON AND SON.
RIVERSIDE, CAMBRIDGE:
PRINTED BY H. O. HOUGHTON AND COMPANY.

CONTENTS OF VOL. VII.

BALLADS AND METRICAL TALES.

VOL. II.

ADVERTISEMENT.

THE two volumes of this collection, which consist of Ballads and Metrical Tales, contain the author's earliest and latest productions of that kind; those which were written with most facility and most glee, and those upon which most time and pains were bestowed, according to the subject and the mode of treating it.

The "Tale of Paraguay" was published separately in 1825, having been so long in hand that the Dedication was written many years before the poem was completed.

"All for Love," and the "Legend of a Cock and a Hen," were published together in a little volume in 1829.

A TALE OF PARAGUAY.

PREFACE.

One of my friends observed to me, in a letter, that many stories which are said to be *founded* on fact have in reality been *foundered* on it. This is the case if there be any gross violation committed or ignorance betrayed of historical manners in the prominent parts of a narrative wherein the writer affects to observe them, or when the groundwork is taken from some part of history so popular and well known that any mixture of fiction disturbs the sense of truth; still more so if the subject be in itself so momentous that any alloy of invention must of necessity debase it: but most of all in themes drawn from Scripture, whether from the more familiar or the more awful portions; for, when what is true is sacred, whatever may be added to it is so surely felt to be false that it appears profane.

Founded on fact the poem is, which is here committed to the world; but, whatever may be its defects, it is liable to none of these objections. The story is so singular, so simple, and withal so complete, that it must have been injured by any alteration. How faithfully it has been followed, the reader may perceive, if he chooses to consult the abridged translation of Dobrizhoffer's "History of the Abipones."

TO EDITH MAY SOUTHEY.

1.

EDITH! ten years are numbered, since the day
Which ushers in the cheerful month of May,
To us by thy dear birth, my daughter dear,
Was blest. Thou therefore didst the name partake
Of that sweet month, the sweetest of the year;
But fitlier was it given thee for the sake
Of a good man, thy father's friend sincere,
Who at the font made answer in thy name.
Thy love and reverence rightly may he claim;
For closely hath he been with me allied
In friendship's holy bonds, from that first hour
When in our youth we met on Tejo's side, —
Bonds which, defying now all Fortune's power,
Time hath not loosened, nor will Death divide.

2.

A child more welcome, by indulgent Heaven
Never to parents' tears and prayers was given;
For scarcely eight months at thy happy birth
Had passed, since of thy sister we were left, —
Our first-born and our only babe, bereft.
Too fair a flower was she for this rude earth!

The features of her beauteous infancy
Have faded from me like a passing cloud,
Or like the glories of an evening sky;
And seldom hath my tongue pronounced her name
Since she was summoned to a happier sphere.
But that dear love, so deeply wounded then,
I in my soul with silent faith sincere
Devoutly cherish till we meet again.

3.

I saw thee first with trembling thankfulness,
O daughter of my hopes and of my fears!
Pressed on thy senseless cheek a troubled kiss,
And breathed my blessing over thee with tears.
But memory did not long our bliss alloy:
For gentle nature, who had given relief,
Weaned with new love the chastened heart from grief;
And the sweet season ministered to joy.

4.

It was a season when their leaves and flowers
The trees as to an Arctic summer spread;
When chilling wintry winds and snowy showers,
Which had too long usurped the vernal hours,
Like spectres from the sight of morning, fled
Before the presence of that joyous May;
And groves and gardens all the live-long day
Rung with the birds' loud love-songs. Over all,
One thrush was heard from morn till even-fall:

Thy Mother well remembers, when she lay
The happy prisoner of the genial bed,
How from yon lofty poplar's topmost spray,
At earliest dawn, his thrilling pipe was heard;
And, when the light of evening died away,
That blithe and indefatigable bird
Still his redundant song of joy and love preferred.

5.

How I have doted on thine infant smiles
At morning, when thine eyes unclosed on mine;
How, as the months in swift succession rolled,
I marked thy human faculties unfold,
And watched the dawning of the light divine;
And with what artifice of playful guiles
Won from thy lips with still-repeated wiles
Kiss after kiss, a reckoning often told,—
Something I ween thou know'st; for thou hast seen
Thy sisters in their turn such fondness prove,
And felt how childhood, in its winning years,
The attempered soul to tenderness can move.
This thou canst tell; but not the hopes and fears
With which a parent's heart doth overflow,—
The thoughts and cares inwoven with that love:
Its nature and its depth, thou dost not, canst not, know.

6.

The years which since thy birth have passed away
May well to thy young retrospect appear

A measureless extent: like yesterday
To me, so soon they filled their short career.
To thee discourse of reason have they brought,
With sense of time and change; and something too
Of this precarious state of things have taught,
Where Man abideth never in one stay;
And of mortality a mournful thought.
And I have seen thine eyes suffused in grief,
When I have said that with autumnal gray
The touch of eld hath marked thy father's head;
That even the longest day of life is brief,
And mine is falling fast into the yellow leaf.

7.

Thy happy nature from the painful thought
With instinct turns, and scarcely canst thou bear
To hear me name the Grave. Thou knowest not
How large a portion of my heart is there!
The faces which I loved in infancy
Are gone; and bosom-friends of riper age,
With whom I fondly talked of years to come,
Summoned before me to their heritage,
Are in the better world, beyond the tomb.
And I have brethren there, and sisters dear,
And dearer babes. I therefore needs must dwell
Often in thought with those whom still I love so well.

8.

Thus wilt thou feel in thy maturer mind:
When grief shall be thy portion, thou wilt find

Safe consolation in such thoughts as these, —
A present refuge in affliction's hour;
And, if indulgent Heaven thy lot should bless
With all imaginable happiness,
Here shalt thou have, my child, beyond all power
Of chance, thy holiest, surest, best delight.
Take therefore now thy Father's latest lay, —
Perhaps his last, — and treasure in thine heart
The feelings that its musing strains convey.
A song it is of life's declining day,
Yet meet for youth. Vain passions to excite,
No strains of morbid sentiment I sing,
Nor tell of idle loves with ill-spent breath:
A reverent offering to the Grave I bring,
And twine a garland for the brow of Death.

KESWICK, 1814.

PROEM.

THAT was a memorable day for Spain,
When on Pamplona's towers, so basely won,
The Frenchmen stood, and saw upon the plain
Their long-expected succors hastening on:
Exultingly they marked the brave array,
And deemed their leader should his purpose gain,
Though Wellington and England barred the way.
Anon the bayonets glittered in the sun,

And frequent cannon flashed, whose lurid light
Reddened through sulphurous smoke; fast volleying round
Rolled the war-thunders, and with long rebound
Backward from many a rock and cloud-capt height
In answering peals Pyrene sent the sound.
Impatient for relief, toward the fight
The angry garrison their eye-balls strain:
Vain was the Frenchman's skill, his valor vain;
And even then, when eager hope almost
Had moved their irreligious lips to prayer,
Averting from the fatal scene their sight,
They breathed the execrations of despair.
For Wellesley's star had risen ascendant there:
Once more he drove the host of France to flight,
And triumphed once again for God and for the right.

That was a day, whose influence far and wide
The struggling nations felt; it was a joy
Wherewith all Europe rung from side to side.
Yet hath Pamplona seen, in former time,
A moment big with mightier consequence,
Affecting many an age and distant clime.
That day it was which saw in her defence,
Contending with the French before her wall,
A noble soldier of Guipuzcoa fall,
Sore hurt, but not to death. For when long care
Restored his shattered leg, and set him free,
He would not brook a slight deformity,
As one who, being gay and debonnair,

In courts conspicuous as in camps must be:
So he, forsooth, a shapely boot must wear;
And the vain man, with peril of his life,
Laid the recovered limb again beneath the knife.

Long time upon the bed of pain he lay,
Whiling with books the weary hours away;
And from that circumstance and this vain man
A train of long events their course began,
Whose term it is not given us yet to see.
Who hath not heard Loyola's sainted name,
Before whom Kings and Nations bowed the knee?
Thy annals, Ethiopia, might proclaim
What deeds arose from that prolific day;
And of dark plots might shuddering Europe tell.
But Science, too, her trophies would display;
Faith give the martyrs of Japan their fame;
And Charity on works of love would dwell
In California's dolorous regions drear;
And where, amid a pathless world of wood,
Gathering a thousand rivers on his way,
Huge Orellana rolls his affluent flood;
And where the happier sons of Paraguay,
By gentleness and pious art subdued,
Bowed their meek heads beneath the Jesuits' sway,
And lived and died in filial servitude.

I love thus uncontrolled, as in a dream,
To muse upon the course of human things;

Exploring sometimes the remotest springs,
Far as tradition lends one guiding gleam;
Or following, upon Thought's audacious wings,
Into Futurity, the endless stream.
But now, in quest of no ambitious height,
I go where Truth and Nature lead my way;
And, ceasing here from desultory flight,
In measured strains I tell a Tale of Paraguay.

CANTO I.

1.

JENNER! for ever shall thy honored name
Among the children of mankind be blest,
Who by thy skill hast taught us how to tame
One dire disease, — the lamentable pest
Which Africa sent forth to scourge the West,
As if in vengeance for her sable brood
So many an age remorselessly oppressed.
For that most fearful malady subdued
Receive a poet's praise, a father's gratitude.

2.

Fair promise be this triumph of an age
When Man, with vain desires no longer blind,
And wise though late, his only war shall wage
Against the miseries which afflict mankind,

Striving with virtuous heart and strenuous mind
Till evil from the earth shall pass away.
Lo, this his glorious destiny assigned!
For that blest consummation let us pray,
And trust in fervent faith, and labor as we may.

3.

The hideous malady, which lost its power
When Jenner's art the dire contagion stayed,
Among Columbia's sons, in fatal hour
Across the wide Atlantic wave conveyed,
Its fiercest form of pestilence displayed:
Where'er its deadly course the plague began,
Vainly the wretched sufferer looked for aid;
Parent from child and child from parent ran,
For tyrannous fear dissolved all natural bonds of man.

4.

A feeble nation of Guarani race,
Thinned by perpetual wars, but unsubdued,
Had taken up at length a resting-place
Among those tracts of lake and swamp and wood,
Where Mondai, issuing from its solitude,
Flows with slow stream to Empalado's bed.
It was a region desolate and rude:
But thither had the horde for safety fled;
And, being there concealed, in peace their lives they led.

5.

There had the tribe a safe asylum found
Amid those marshes wide and woodlands dense,
With pathless wilds and waters spread around,
And labyrinthine swamps, — a sure defence
From human foes, but not from pestilence.
The spotted plague appeared, that direst ill;
How brought among them none could tell, or
whence;
The mortal seed had lain among them still,
And quickened now to work the Lord's mysterious
will.

6.

Alas! it was no medicable grief
Which herbs might reach; nor could the jug-
gler's power,
With all his antic mummeries, bring relief:
Faith might not aid him in that ruling hour,
Himself a victim now. The dreadful stour
None could escape, nor aught its force assuage.
The marriageable maiden had her dower [rage,
From Death; the strong man sunk beneath its
And Death cut short the thread of childhood and of
age.

7.

No time for customary mourning now;
With hand close-clinched to pluck the rooted hair,

To beat the bosom, on the swelling brow
Inflict redoubled blows, and blindly tear
The cheeks, indenting bloody furrows there,
The deep-traced signs indelible of woe;
Then to some crag, or bank abrupt, repair,
And, giving grief its scope, infuriate throw
The impatient body thence upon the earth below.

8.

Devices these by poor weak nature taught,
Which thus a change of suffering would obtain,
And, flying from intolerable thought
And piercing recollections, would full fain
Distract itself by sense of fleshly pain
From anguish that the soul must else endure.
Easier all outward torments to sustain [cure,
Than those heart-wounds which only time can
And He in whom alone the hopes of man are sure.

9.

None sorrowed here; the sense of woe was seared,
When every one endured his own sore ill.
The prostrate sufferers neither hoped nor feared;
The body labored, but the heart was still:
So let the conquering malady fulfil
Its fatal course, rest cometh at the end!
Passive they lay, with neither wish nor will
For aught but this; nor did they long attend
That welcome boon from Death, the never-failing
friend.

10.

Who is there to make ready now the pit,
The house that will content from this day forth
Its easy tenant? Who in vestments fit
Shall swathe the sleeper for his bed of earth,
Now tractable as when a babe at birth?
Who now the ample funeral urn shall knead,
And, burying it beneath his proper hearth,
Deposit there with careful hands the dead,
And lightly then relay the floor above his head?

11.

Unwept, unshrouded, and unsepulchred,
The hammock, where they hang, for winding-sheet
And grave suffices the deserted dead;
There from the armadillo's searching feet
Safer than if within the tomb's retreat.
The carrion birds obscene in vain essay
To find that quarry: round and round they beat
The air, but fear to enter for their prey;
And from the silent door the jaguar turns away.

12.

But Nature for her universal law
Hath other, surer instruments in store,
Whom from the haunts of men no wonted awe
Withholds as with a spell. In swarms they pour
From wood and swamp; and, when their work is o'er,

On the white bones the mouldering roof will fall;
Seeds will take root, and spring in sun and shower;
And Mother Earth ere long with her green pall,
Resuming to herself the wreck, will cover all.

13.

Oh! better thus with earth to have their part,
Than in Egyptian catacombs to lie,
Age after age preserved by horrid art,
In ghastly image of humanity!
Strange pride that with corruption thus would vie!
And strange delusion that would thus maintain
The fleshly form till cycles shall pass by,
And, in the series of the eternal chain,
The spirit come to seek its old abode again!

14.

One pair alone survived the general fate;
Left in such drear and mournful solitude,
That death might seem a preferable state.
Not more depressed the Arkite patriarch stood,
When landing first on Ararat he viewed,
Where all around the mountain summits lay,
Like islands seen amid the boundless flood;
Nor our first parents more forlorn than they,
Through Eden when they took their solitary way.

15.

Alike to them, it seemed in their despair,
Whither they wandered from the infected spot.

Chance might direct their steps: they took no
care;
Come well or ill to them, it mattered not!
Left as they were in that unhappy lot,
The sole survivors they of all their race,
They recked not when their fate, nor where, nor
In this resignment to their hopeless case, [what,
Indifferent to all choice or circumstance of place.

16.

That palsying stupor passed away ere long;
And, as the spring of health resumed its power,
They felt that life was dear, and hope was strong.
What marvel? 'Twas with them the morning hour,
When bliss appears to be the natural dower
Of all the creatures of this joyous earth;
And sorrow, fleeting, like a vernal shower,
Scarce interrupts the current of our mirth:
Such is the happy heart we bring with us at birth.

17.

Though of his nature and his boundless love
Erring, yet, tutored by instinctive sense,
They rightly deemed the Power who rules above
Had saved them from the wasting pestilence.
That favoring Power would still be their defence:
Thus were they by their late deliverance taught
To place a childlike trust in Providence;
And in their state forlorn they found this thought
Of natural faith with hope and consolation fraught.

18.

And now they built themselves a leafy bower,
Amid a glade, slow Mondai's stream beside,
Screened from the southern blast of piercing power;
Not like their native dwelling, long and wide,
By skilful toil of numbers edified,
The common home of all, their human nest,
Where threescore hammocks, pendent side by side,
Were ranged, and on the ground the fires were dressed:
Alas! that populous hive hath now no living guest!

19.

A few firm stakes they planted in the ground,
Circling a narrow space, yet large enow;
These, strongly interknit, they closed around
With basket-work of many a pliant bough.
The roof was like the sides; the door was low,
And rude the hut, and trimmed with little care,
For little heart had they to dress it now;
Yet was the humble structure fresh and fair,
And soon its inmates found that love might sojourn there.

20.

Quiara could recall to mind the course
Of twenty summers; perfectly he knew

Whate'er his fathers taught of skill or force.
Right to the mark his whizzing lance he threw,
And from his bow the unerring arrow flew
With fatal aim; and, when the laden bee
Buzzed by him in its flight, he could pursue
Its path with certain ken, and follow free
Until he traced the hive in hidden bank or tree.

21.

Of answering years was Monnema, nor less
Expert in all her sex's household ways.
The Indian weed she skilfully could dress;
And in what depth to drop the yellow maize
She knew, and when around its stem to raise
The lightened soil; and well could she prepare
Its ripened seed for food, her proper praise;
Or in the embers turn with frequent care
Its succulent head yet green, sometimes for daintier fare.

22.

And how to macerate the bark she knew,
And draw apart its beaten fibres fine,
And, bleaching them in sun and air and dew,
From dry and glossy filaments intwine,
With rapid twirl of hand, the lengthening line;
Next interknitting well the twisted thread,
In many an even mesh its knots combine,
And shape in tapering length the pensile bed,
Light hammock there to hang beneath the leafy shed.

23.

Time had been when, expert in works of clay,
She lent her hands the swelling urn to mould,
And filled it for the appointed festal day
With the belovèd beverage which the bold
Quaffed in their triumph and their joy of old;
The fruitful cause of many an uproar rude,
When, in their drunken bravery uncontrolled,
Some bitter jest awoke the dormant feud,
And wrath and rage and strife and wounds and death ensued.

24.

These occupations were gone by; the skill
Was useless now, which once had been her pride.
Content were they, when thirst impelled, to fill
The dry and hollow gourd from Mondai's side;
The river from its sluggish bed supplied
A draught for repetition all unmeet;
Howbeit the bodily want was satisfied;
No feverish pulse ensued, nor ireful heat;
Their days were undisturbed, their natural sleep was sweet.

25.

She, too, had learned in youth how best to trim
The honored Chief for his triumphal day,
And, covering with soft gums the obedient limb
And body, then with feathers overlay,

In regular hues disposed, a rich display.
Well pleased the glorious savage stood, and eyed
The growing work; then, vain of his array,
Looked with complacent frown from side to side,
Stalked with elater step, and swelled with statelier pride.

26.

Feasts and carousals, vanity and strife,
Could have no place with them in solitude
To break the tenor of their even life.
Quiara day by day his game pursued,
Searching the air, the water, and the wood,
With hawk-like eye, and arrow sure as fate;
And Monnema prepared the hunter's food:
Cast with him here in this forlorn estate,
In all things for the man was she a fitting mate.

27.

The Moon had gathered oft her monthly store
Of light, and oft in darkness left the sky,
Since Monnema a growing burden bore
Of life and hope. The appointed weeks go by;
And now her hour is come, and none is nigh
To help: but human help she needed none.
A few short throes endured with scarce a cry,
Upon the bank she laid her new-born son,
Then slid into the stream, and bathed, and all was done.

28.

Might old observances have there been kept,
Then should the husband to that pensile bed,
Like one exhausted with the birth, have crept,
And, laying down in feeble guise his head,
For many a day been nursed and dieted
With tender care, to childing mothers due.
Certes a custom strange, and yet far spread
Through many a savage tribe, howe'er it grew,
And once in the Old World known as widely as the
New.

29.

This could not then be done; he might not lay
The bow and those unerring shafts aside;
Nor through the appointed weeks forego the prey,
Still to be sought amid those regions wide,
None being there who should the while provide
That lonely household with their needful food:
So, still Quiara through the forest plied
His daily task, and in the thickest wood
Still laid his snares for birds, and still the chase
pursued.

30.

But seldom may such thoughts of mingled joy
A father's agitated breast dilate,
As when he first beheld that infant boy.
Who hath not proved it, ill can estimate

The feeling of that stirring hour, — the weight
Of that new sense, the thoughtful, pensive bliss.
In all the changes of our changeful state,
Even from the cradle to the grave, I wis,
The heart doth undergo no change so great as this.

31.

A deeper and unwonted feeling filled
These parents, gazing on their new-born son.
Already in their busy hopes they build
On this frail sand. Now let the seasons run,
And let the natural work of time be done
With them: for unto them a child is born;
And, when the hand of Death may reach the one,
The other will not now be left to mourn,
A solitary wretch, all utterly forlorn.

32.

Thus Monnema and thus Quiara thought,
Though each the melancholy thought repressed:
They could not choose but feel, yet uttered not
The human feeling, which in hours of rest
Would often rise, and fill the boding breast
With a dread foretaste of that mournful day,
When, at the inexorable Power's behest,
The unwilling spirit, called perforce away,
Must leave, for ever leave, its dear connatural clay.

33.

Linked as they were, where each to each was all,
How might the poor survivor hope to bear

That heaviest loss which one day must befall,
Nor sink beneath the weight of his despair?
Scarce could the heart even for a moment dare
That miserable time to cóntemplate,
When the dread Messenger should find them there,
From whom is no escape, — and reckless Fate,
Whom it had bound so close, for ever separate.

34.

Lighter that burden lay upon the heart
When this dear babe was born to share their lot;
They could endure to think that they must part.
Then, too, a glad consolatory thought
Arose, while, gazing on the child, they sought
With hope their dreary prospect to delude,
Till they almost believed, as fancy taught,
How that from them a tribe should spring renewed,
To people and possess that ample solitude.

35.

Such hope they felt, but felt that, whatsoe'er
The undiscoverable to come might prove,
Unwise it were to let that bootless care
Disturb the present hours of peace and love.
For they had gained a happiness above
The state which in their native horde was known:
No outward causes were there here to move
Discord and alien thoughts; being thus alone
From all mankind, their hearts and their desires were one.

36.

Different their love in kind and in degree
From what their poor depraved forefathers knew,
With whom degenerate instincts were left free
To take their course, and blindly to pursue,
Unheeding they the ills that must ensue,
The bent of brute desire. No mortal tie
Bound the hard husband to his servile crew
Of wives; and they the chance of change might try,
All love destroyed by such preposterous liberty.

37.

Far other tie this solitary pair
Indissolubly bound; true helpmates they,
In joy or grief, in weal or woe to share,
In sickness or in health, through life's long day;
And, re-assuming in their hearts her sway,
Benignant Nature made the burden light.
It was the Woman's pleasure to obey,
The Man's to ease her toil in all he might;
So each, in serving each, obtained the best delight.

38.

And as connubial, so parental love
Obeyed unerring Nature's order here;
For now no force of impious custom strove
Against her law, — such as was wont to sear
The unhappy heart with usages severe,
Till hardened mothers in the grave could lay

Their living babes with no compunctious tear;
So monstrous men become, when from the way
Of primal light they turn through heathen paths
astray.

39.

Delivered from this yoke, in them henceforth
The springs of natural love may freely flow:
New joys, new virtues, with that happy birth
Are born, and with the growing infant grow.
Source of our purest happiness below
Is that benignant law which hath intwined
Dearest delight with strongest duty, so
That in the healthy heart and righteous mind
Ever they co-exist, inseparably combined.

40.

Oh! bliss for them when in that infant face
They now the unfolding faculties descry,
And, fondly gazing, trace, or think they trace,
The first faint speculation in that eye
Which hitherto hath rolled in vacancy!
Oh! bliss in that soft countenance to seek
Some mark of recognition, and espy
The quiet smile which in the innocent cheek
Of kindness and of kind its consciousness doth speak!

41.

For him, if born among their native tribe,
Some haughty name his parents had thought good,

As weening that therewith they should ascribe
The strength of some fierce tenant of the wood,
The water, or the aërial solitude,
Jaguar or vulture, water-wolf or snake,
The beast that prowls abroad in search of blood,
Or reptile that within the treacherous brake
Waits for the prey, upcoiled, its hunger to aslake.

42.

Now softened as their spirits were by love,
Abhorrent from such thoughts they turned away;
And with a happier feeling, from the dove,
They named the child Yeruti. On a day,
When, smiling at his mother's breast in play,
They in his tones of murmuring pleasure heard
A sweet resemblance of the stock-dove's lay,
Fondly they named him from that gentle bird;
And soon such happy use endeared the fitting word.

43.

Days pass, and moons have waxed and waned, and still
This dovelet, nestled in their leafy bower,
Obtains increase of sense and strength and will,
As in due order many a latent power
Expands, — humanity's exalted dower;
And they, while thus the days serenely fled,
Beheld him flourish like a vigorous flower,
Which, lifting from a genial soil its head,
By seasonable suns and kindly showers is fed.

44.

Ere long the cares of helpless babyhood
To the next stage of infancy give place, —
That age with sense of conscious growth endued,
When every gesture hath its proper grace:
Then come the unsteady step, the tottering pace;
And watchful hopes and emulous thoughts appear;
The imitative lips essay to trace
Their words, observant both with eye and ear,
In mutilated sounds which parents love to hear.

45.

Serenely thus the seasons pass away;
And, oh! how rapidly they seem to fly
With those for whom to-morrow, like to-day,
Glides on in peaceful uniformity!
Five years have since Yeruti's birth gone by,
Five happy years; and ere the Moon, which then
Hung like a Sylphid's light canoe on high,
Should fill its circle, Monnema again,
Laying her burden down, must bear a mother's pain.

46.

Alas! a keener pang, before that day,
Must by the wretched Monnema be borne!
In quest of game, Quiara went his way
To roam the wilds, as he was wont, one morn:
She looked in vain at eve for his return.
By moonlight, through the midnight solitude,

She sought him; and she found his garment torn,
His bow and useless arrows in the wood,
Marks of a jaguar's feet, a broken spear, and blood.

CANTO II.

1.

O THOU who, listening to the Poet's song,
Dost yield thy willing spirit to his sway!
Look not that I should painfully prolong
The sad narration of that fatal day
With tragic details; all too true the lay!
Nor is my purpose e'er to entertain
The heart with useless grief; but, as I may,
Blend in my calm and meditative strain
Consolatory thoughts, the balm for real pain.

2.

O Youth or Maiden, whosoe'er thou art,
Safe in my guidance may thy spirit be!
I wound not wantonly the tender heart;
And if sometimes a tear of sympathy
Should rise, it will from bitterness be free,—
Yea, with a healing virtue be endued,
As thou, in this true tale, shalt hear from me
Of evils overcome, and grief subdued,
And virtues springing up like flowers in solitude.

3.

The unhappy Monnema, when thus bereft,
Sunk not beneath the desolating blow
Widowed she was: but still her child was left;
For him must she sustain the weight of woe,
Which else would in that hour have laid her low.
Nor wished she now the work of death complete:
Then only doth the soul of woman know
Its proper strength, when love and duty meet;
Invincible the heart wherein they have their seat.

4.

The seamen who, upon some coral reef,
Are cast amid the interminable main,
Still cling to life, and, hoping for relief,
Drag on their days of wretchedness and pain.
In turtle-shells they hoard the scanty rain,
And eat its flesh, sun-dried for lack of fire,
Till the weak body can no more sustain
Its wants, but sinks beneath its sufferings dire;
Most miserable man who sees the rest expire!

5.

He lingers there while months and years go by,
And holds his hope though months and years have passed;
And still at morning round the farthest sky,
And still at eve, his eagle glance is cast,
If there he may behold the far-off mast
Arise, for which he hath not ceased to pray.

And if perchance a ship should come at last,
And bear him from that dismal bank away,
He blesses God that he hath lived to see that day.

6.

So strong a hold hath life upon the soul,
Which sees no dawning of eternal light,
But subject to this mortal frame's control,
Forgetful of its origin and right,
Content in bondage dwells and utter night.
By worthier ties was this poor mother bound
To life: even while her grief was at the height,
Then in maternal love support she found,
And in maternal cares a healing for her wound.

7.

For now her hour is come: a girl is born,
Poor infant, all unconscious of its fate,
How passing strange, how utterly forlorn!
The genial season served to mitigate,
In all it might, their sorrowful estate,
Supplying to the mother, at her door,
From neighboring trees, which bent beneath their weight,
A full supply of fruitage now mature;
So in that time of need their sustenance was sure.

8.

Nor then alone, but alway, did the Eye
Of Mercy look upon that lonely bower.

Days passed, and weeks and months and years went by,
And never evil thing the while had power
To enter there. The boy, in sun and shower,
Rejoicing in his strength, to youthhed grew;
And Mooma, that belovèd girl, a dower
Of gentleness from bounteous nature drew,
With all that should the heart of womankind imbue.

9.

The tears which o'er her infancy were shed
Profuse resented not of grief alone:
Maternal love their bitterness allayed,
And, with a strength and virtue all its own,
Sustained the breaking heart. A look, a tone,
A gesture of that innocent babe, in eyes
With saddest recollections overflown,
Would sometimes make a tender smile arise,
Like sunshine opening through a shower in vernal skies.

10.

No looks but those of tenderness were found
To turn upon that helpless infant dear;
And, as her sense unfolded, never sound
Of wrath or discord brake upon her ear.
Her soul its native purity sincere
Possessed, by no example here defiled:
From envious passions free, exempt from fear,
Unknowing of all ill, amid the wild
Beloving and beloved she grew, a happy child.

11.

Yea, where that solitary bower was placed,
Though all unlike to Paradise the scene,
(A wide circumference of woodlands waste,)
Something of what in Eden might have been
Was shadowed there imperfectly, I ween,
In this fair creature: safe from all offence,
Expanding like a sheltered plant serene,
Evils that fret and stain being far from thence,
Her heart in peace and joy retained its innocence.

12.

At first the infant to Yeruti proved
A cause of wonder and disturbing joy.
A stronger tie than that of kindred moved
His inmost being, as the happy boy
Felt in his heart of hearts, without alloy,
The sense of kind: a fellow-creature she,
In whom, when now she ceased to be a toy
For tender sport, his soul rejoiced to see
Connatural powers expand, and growing sympathy.

13.

For her he culled the fairest flowers, and sought
Throughout the woods the earliest fruits for her.
The cayman's eggs, the honeycomb, he brought
To this belovèd sister, — whatsoe'er,
To his poor thought, of delicate or rare
The wilds might yield, solicitous to find.

They who affirm all natural acts declare
Self-love to be the ruler of the mind,
Judge from their own mean hearts, and foully wrong
mankind.

14.

Three souls in whom no selfishness had place
Were here,—three happy souls, which undefiled,
Albeit in darkness, still retained a trace
Of their celestial origin. The wild
Was as a sanctuary, where Nature smiled
Upon these simple children of her own,
And, cherishing whate'er was meek and mild,
Called forth the gentle virtues, such alone,
The evils which evoke the stronger being unknown.

15.

What though at birth we bring with us the seed
Of sin, a mortal taint,—in heart and will
Too surely felt, too plainly shown in deed,—
Our fatal heritage; yet are we still
The children of the All-Merciful; and ill
They teach who tell us that from hence must flow
God's wrath, and then, his justice to fulfil,
Death everlasting, never-ending woe:
Oh miserable lot of man, if it were so!

16.

Falsely and impiously teach they who thus
Our heavenly Father's holy will misread!

In bounty hath the Lord created us,
In love redeemed. From this authentic creed
Let no bewildering sophistry impede
The heart's entire assent; for God is good.
Hold firm this faith, and, in whatever need,
Doubt not but thou wilt find thy soul endued
With all-sufficing strength of heavenly fortitude.

17.

By nature peccable and frail are we,
Easily beguiled; to vice, to error, prone;
But apt for virtue too. Humanity
Is not a field where tares and thorns alone
Are left to spring: good seed hath there been sown
With no unsparing hand. Sometimes the shoot
Is choked with weeds, or withers on a stone;
But in a kindly soil it strikes its root,
And flourisheth, and bringeth forth abundant fruit.

18.

Love, duty, generous feeling, tenderness,
Spring in the uncontaminated mind;
And these were Mooma's natural dower. Nor less
Had liberal Nature to the boy assigned;
Happier herein than if among mankind
Their lot had fallen, — oh, certes, happier here!
That all things tended still more close to bind
Their earliest ties, and they from year to year
Retained a childish heart, fond, simple, and sincere.

19.

They had no sad reflection to alloy
The calm contentment of the passing day,
Nor foresight to disturb the present joy.
Not so with Monnema : albeit the sway
Of time had reached her heart, and worn away,
At length, the grief so deeply seated there,
The future often, like a burden, lay
Upon that heart, a cause of secret care
And melancholy thought; yet did she not despair.

20.

Chance from the fellowship of human-kind
Had cut them off, and chance might re-unite.
On this poor possibility her mind
Reposed; she did not for herself invite
The unlikely thought, and cherish with delight
The dream of what such change might haply bring:
Gladness with hope long since had taken flight
From her; she felt that life was on the wing,
And happiness, like youth, has here no second spring.

21.

So were her feelings to her lot composed,
That to herself all change had now been pain:
For Time upon her own desires had closed;
But, in her children as she lived again,
For their dear sake she learnt to entertain
A wish for human intercourse renewed;

And oftentimes, while they devoured the strain.
Would she beguile their evening solitude
With stories strangely told and strangely understood.

22.

Little she knew; for little had she seen,
And little of traditionary lore
Had reached her ear; and yet to them, I ween,
Their mother's knowledge seemed a boundless store.
A world it opened to their thoughts; yea, more, —
Another world beyond this mortal state.
Bereft of her, they had indeed been poor;
Being left to animal sense, degenerate,
Mere creatures, they had sunk below the beasts' estate.

23.

The human race, from her they understood,
Was not within that lonely hut confined;
But distant far, beyond their world of wood,
Were tribes and powerful nations of their kind;
And of the old observances which bind
People and chiefs, the ties of man and wife,
The laws of kin religiously assigned,
Rites, customs, scenes of riotry and strife,
And all the strange vicissitudes of savage life.

24.

Wondering they listen to the wondrous tale;
But no repining thought such tales excite:

Only a wish, if wishes might avail,
Was haply felt, with juvenile delight,
To mingle in the social dance at night,
Where the broad moonshine, level as a flood,
O'erspread the plain, and in the silver light,
Well pleased, the placid elders sate and viewed
The sport, and seemed therein to feel their youth
renewed.

25.

But when the darker scenes their mother drew, —
What crimes were wrought when drunken fury
raged;
What miseries from their fatal discord grew,
When horde with horde in deadly strife engaged;
The rancorous hate with which their wars they
waged;
The more unnatural horrors which ensued,
When, with inveterate vengeance unassuaged,
The victors round their slaughtered captives stood,
And babes were brought to dip their little hands in
blood, —

26.

Horrent they heard; and with her hands the Maid
Pressed her eyes close, as if she strove to blot
The hateful image which her mind portrayed.
The Boy sate silently, intent in thought;
Then with a deep-drawn sigh, as if he sought
To heave the oppressive feeling from his breast,

Complacently compared their harmless lot
With such wild life, outrageous and unblest;
Securely thus to live, he said, was surely best.

27.

On tales of blood they could not bear to dwell;
From such their hearts abhorrent shrunk in fear.
Better they liked that Monnema should tell
Of things unseen ; what Power had placed them here,
And whence the living spirit came, and where
It passed when parted from this mortal mould:
Of such mysterious themes with willing ear
They heard, devoutly listening while she told
Strangely disfigured truths, and fables feigned of old.

28.

By the Great Spirit man was made, she said;
His voice it was which pealed along the sky,
And shook the heavens, and filled the earth with dread.
Alone and inaccessible, on high
He had his dwelling-place eternally,
And Father was his name. This all knew well:
But none had seen his face; and if his eye
Regarded what upon the earth befell,
Or if he cared for man, she knew not: who could tell?

29.

But this, she said, was sure, — that after death
There was reward, and there was punishment;

And that the evil-doers, when the breath
Of their injurious lives at length was spent,
Into all noxious forms abhorred were sent
Of beasts and reptiles: so retaining still
Their old propensities, on evil bent,
They worked where'er they might their wicked will,
The natural foes of man, whom we pursue and kill.

30.

Of better spirits, some there were who said
That in the grave they had their place of rest.
Lightly they laid the earth upon the dead,
Lest in his narrow tenement the guest
Should suffer underneath such load oppressed.
But that death surely set the spirit free,
Sad proof to them poor Monnema addressed,
Drawn from their father's fate; no grave had he
Wherein his soul might dwell: this, therefore, could not be.

31.

Likelier they taught who said that to the Land
Of Souls the happy spirit took its flight, —
A region underneath the sole command
Of the Good Power; by him for the upright
Appointed, and replenished with delight;
A land where nothing evil ever came,
Sorrow nor pain nor peril nor affright
Nor change nor death; but there the human frame,
Untouched by age or ill, continued still the same.

32.

Winds would not pierce it there, nor heat and cold
Grieve, nor thirst parch, and hunger pine; but there
The sun by day its even influence hold
With genial warmth, and through the unclouded air
The moon upon her nightly journey fare:
The lakes and fish-full streams are never dry;
Trees, ever green, perpetual fruitage bear;
And, wheresoe'er the hunter turns his eye,
Water and earth and heaven to him their stores supply.

33.

And once there was a way to that good land;
For in mid-earth a wondrous Tree there grew,
By which the adventurer might, with foot and hand,
From branch to branch his upward course pursue, —
An easy path, if what were said be true,
Albeit the ascent was long; and, when the height
Was gained, that blissful region was in view,
Wherein the traveller safely might alight,
And roam abroad at will, and take his free delight.

34.

Oh happy time, when ingress thus was given
To the upper world, and at their pleasure they

Whose hearts were strong might pass from Earth
to Heaven
By their own act and choice! In evil day
Mishap had fatally cut off that way;
And none may now the Land of Spirits gain,
Till, from its dear-loved tenement of clay,
Violence or age, infirmity and pain,
Divorce the soul, which there full gladly would
remain.

35.

Such grievous loss had by their own misdeed
Upon the unworthy race of men been brought.
An aged woman once, who could not speed
In fishing, earnestly one day besought
Her countrymen that they of what they caught
A portion would upon her wants bestow.
They set her hunger and her age at nought,
And still to her entreaties answered "No!"
And mocked her, till they made her heart with rage
o'erflow.

36.

But that Old Woman, by such wanton wrong
Inflamed, went hurrying down; and in the pride
Of magic power, wherein the crone was strong,
Her human form infirm she laid aside.
Better the Capiguara's limbs supplied
A strength accordant to her fierce intent:
These she assumed; and, burrowing deep and wide
Beneath the Tree, with vicious will, she went
To inflict upon mankind a lasting punishment.

37.

Downward she wrought her way, and, all around
Laboring, the solid earth she undermined,
And loosened all the roots; then from the ground
Emerging, in her hatred of her kind,
Resumed her proper form, and breathed a wind
Which gathered like a tempest round its head:
Eftsoon the lofty Tree its top inclined,
Uptorn with horrible convulsion dread,
And over half the world its mighty wreck lay spread.

38.

But never scion sprouted from that Tree,
Nor seed sprang up; and thus the easy way,
Which had till then for young and old been free,
Was closed upon the sons of men for aye.
The mighty ruin mouldered where it lay,
Till not a trace was left; and now, in sooth,
Almost had all remembrance passed away.
This from the elders she had heard in youth:
Some said it was a tale, and some a very truth.

39.

Nathless, departed spirits at their will
Could from the Land of Souls pass to and fro:
They come to us in sleep, when all is still, —
Sometimes to warn against the impending blow;
Alas! more oft to visit us in woe:
Though in their presence there was poor relief!

And this had sad experience made her know;
For, when Quiara came, his stay was brief,
And, waking then, she felt a freshened sense of grief.

40.

Yet to behold his face again, and hear
His voice, though painful, was a deep delight:
It was a joy to think that he was near,
To see him in the visions of the night,
To know that the departed still requite
The love which to their memory still will cling;
And, though he might not bless her waking sight
With his dear presence, 'twas a blessèd thing
That sleep would thus sometimes his actual image bring.

41.

"Why comes he not to me?" Yeruti cries;
And Mooma, echoing with a sigh the thought,
Asked why it was that to her longing eyes
No dream the image of her father brought.
Nor Monnema to solve that question sought
In vain, content in ignorance to dwell:
Perhaps it was because they knew him not;
Perhaps, — but, sooth, she could not answer well;
What the departed did, themselves alone could tell.

42.

What one tribe held, another disbelieved;
For all concerning this was dark, she said;

Uncertain all, and hard to be received.
The dreadful race, from whom their fathers fled,
Boasted that even the Country of the Dead
Was theirs; and, where their Spirits chose to go,
The ghosts of other men retired in dread
Before the face of that victorious foe:
No better, then, the world above, than this below!

43.

What then, alas! if this were true, was death?
Only a mournful change from ill to ill!
And some there were who said the living breath
Would ne'er be taken from us by the will
Of the Good Father, but continue still
To feed with life the mortal frame he gave,
Did not mischance or wicked witchcraft kill;
Evils from which no care availed to save,
And whereby all were sent to fill the greedy grave.

44.

In vain to counterwork the baleful charm
By spells of rival witchcraft was it sought;
Less potent was that art to help than harm.
No means of safety old experience brought:
Nor better fortune did they find who thought
From Death, as from some living foe, to fly;
For speed or subterfuge availed them nought,
But, wheresoe'er they fled, they found him nigh:
None ever could elude that unseen enemy.

45.

Bootless the boast, and vain the proud intent,
Of those who hoped, with arrogant display
Of arms and force, to scare him from their tent;
As if their threatful shouts, and fierce array
Of war, could drive the Invisible away!
Sometimes, regardless of the sufferer's groan,
They dragged the dying out, and as a prey
Exposed him, that, content with him alone,
Death might depart, and thus his fate avert their own.

46.

Depart he might, but only to return
In quest of other victims, soon or late;
When they who held this fond belief would learn,
Each by his own inevitable fate,
That, in the course of man's uncertain state,
Death is the one and only certain thing.
Oh folly, then, to fly or deprecate
That which at last Time, ever on the wing,
Certain as day and night, to weary age must bring!

47.

While thus the Matron spake, the youthful twain
Listened in deep attention, wistfully;
Whether with more of wonder or of pain
Uneath it were to tell. With steady eye
Intent they heard; and, when she paused, a sigh
Their sorrowful foreboding seemed to speak:

Questions to which she could not give reply
Yeruti asked; and, for that Maiden meek,
Involuntary tears ran down her quiet cheek.

48.

A different sentiment within them stirred,
When Monnema recalled to mind one day,
Imperfectly, what she had sometimes heard
In childhood, long ago, the Elders say, —
Almost from memory had it passed away, —
How there appeared amid the woodlands men
Whom the Great Spirit sent there to convey
His gracious will; but little heed she then
Had given, and like a dream it now recurred again.

49.

But these young questioners from time to time
Called up the long-forgotten theme anew.
Strange men they were, from some remotest clime,
She said, of different speech, uncouth to view,
Having hair upon their face, and white in hue:
Across the World of waters wide they came
Devotedly the Father's work to do,
And seek the Red Men out, and in his name
His merciful laws and love and promises proclaim.

50.

They served a Maid more beautiful than tongue
Could tell or heart conceive. Of human race,

All heavenly as that Virgin was, she sprung;
But for her beauty and celestial grace,
Being one in whose pure elements no trace
Had e'er inhered of sin or mortal stain,
The highest Heaven was now her dwelling-place;
There as a Queen divine she held her reign,
And there in endless joy for ever would remain.

51.

Her feet upon the crescent Moon were set,
And, moving in their order round her head,
The Stars compose her sparkling coronet.
There at her breast the Virgin Mother fed
A Babe divine, who was to judge the dead;
Such power the Spirit gave this awful Child:
Severe he was, and in his anger dread,
Yet alway at his Mother's will grew mild,
So well did he obey that Maiden undefiled.

52.

Sometimes she had descended from above
To visit her true votaries, and requite
Such as had served her well. And for her love,
These bearded men, forsaking all delight,
With labor long and dangers infinite,
Across the great blue waters came, and sought
The Red Men here, to win them, if they might,
From bloody ways, rejoiced to profit aught,
Even when with their own lives the benefit was bought.

53.

For, trusting in this heavenly Maiden's grace,
It was for them a joyful thing to die,
As men who went to have their happy place
With her, and with that Holy Child, on high,
In fields of bliss above the starry sky,
In glory, at the Virgin Mother's feet;
And all who kept their lessons faithfully
An everlasting guerdon there would meet,
When Death had led their souls to that celestial seat.

54.

On earth they offered, too, an easy life
To those who their mild lessons would obey, —
Exempt from want, from danger, and from strife;
And, from the forest leading them away,
They placed them underneath this Virgin's sway,
A numerous fellowship, in peace to dwell;
Their high and happy office there to pay
Devotions due, which she requited well,
Their heavenly Guardian she in whatsoe'er befell.

55.

Thus, Monnema remembered, it was told
By one who, in his hot and headstrong youth,
Had left her happy service; but, when old,
Lamented oft, with unavailing ruth,
And thoughts which, sharper than a serpent's tooth,
Pierced him, that he had changed that peaceful place

For the fierce freedom and the ways uncouth
Of their wild life, and lost that Lady's grace,
Wherefore he had no hope to see in Heaven her face.

56.

And she remembered, too, when first they fled
For safety to the farthest solitude
Before their cruel foes, and lived in dread
That thither, too, their steps might be pursued
By those old enemies athirst for blood,
How some among them hoped to see the day
When these belovèd messengers of good
To that lone hiding-place might find the way,
And them to their abode of blessedness convey.

57.

Such tales excited in Yeruti's heart
A stirring hope that haply he might meet
Some minister of Heaven; and many a part,
Untrod before, of that wild wood retreat,
Did he, with indefatigable feet,
Explore; yet ever from the fruitless quest
Returned at evening to his native seat
By daily disappointment undepressed,—
So buoyant was the hope that filled his youthful breast.

58.

At length the hour approached that should fulfil
His harmless heart's desire, when they shall see

Their fellow-kind, and take for good or ill
The fearful chance — for such it needs must be —
Of change from that entire simplicity.
Yet wherefore should the thought of change appall?
Grief it perhaps might bring, and injury
And death; but evil never can befall
The virtuous, for the Eye of Heaven is over all.

CANTO III.

1.

Amid those marshy woodlands far and wide,
Which spread beyond the soaring vulture's eye,
There grew, on Empalado's southern side,
Groves of that tree whose leaves adust supply
The Spaniards with their daily luxury;
A beverage whose salubrious use obtains
Through many a land of mines and slavery,
Even over all La Plata's sea-like plains,
And Chili's mountain realm, and proud Peru's domains.

2.

But better for the injured Indian race
Had woods of machineel the land o'erspread:
Yea, in that tree, so blest by Nature's grace,
A direr curse had they inherited

Than if the Upas there had reared its head,
And sent its baneful scions all around,
Blasting where'er its effluent force was shed,
In air and water, and the infected ground,
All things wherein the breath or sap of life is found.

3.

The poor Guaranies dreamt of no such ill,
When, for themselves in miserable hour,
The virtues of that leaf, with pure good-will,
They taught their unsuspected visitor,
New in the land as yet. They learnt his power
Too soon, which law nor conscience could restrain;
A fearless but inhuman conqueror,
Heart-hardened by the accursèd lust of gain:
Oh fatal thirst of gold! oh foul reproach for Spain!

4.

For gold and silver had the Spaniards sought,
Exploring Paraguay with desperate pains;
Their way through forests, axe in hand, they wrought;
Drenched from above by unremitting rains,
They waded over inundated plains,
Forward by hope of plunder still allured;
So they might one day count their golden gains,
They cared not at what cost of sin procured;
All dangers they defied, all sufferings they endured.

5.

Barren alike of glory and of gold
That region proved to them; nor would the soil
Unto their unindustrious hands unfold
Harvests, the fruit of peace, and wine and oil,—
The treasures that repay contented toil
With health and weal; treasures that with them bring
No guilt for priest and penance to assoil,
Nor with their venom arm the awakened sting
Of conscience at that hour when life is vanishing.

6.

But, keen of eye in their pursuit of gain,
The conquerors looked for lucre in this tree:
An annual harvest there might they attain,
Without the cost of annual industry.
'Twas but to gather in what there grew free,
And share Potosi's wealth. Nor thence alone,
But gold in glad exchange they soon should see
From all that once the Incas called their own,
Or where the Zippa's power or Zaque's laws were known.

7.

For this, in fact, though not in name, a slave,
The Indian from his family was torn;
And droves on droves were sent to find a grave
In woods and swamps, by toil severe outworn,—
No friend at hand to succor or to mourn,
In death unpitied, as in life unblest.

Oh miserable race, to slavery born!
Yet, when we look beyond this world's unrest,
More miserable then the oppressors than the oppressed.

8.

Often had Kings essayed to check the ill
By edicts not so well enforced as meant:
A present power was wanting to fulfil
Remote authority's sincere intent.
To Avarice, on its present purpose bent,
The voice of distant Justice spake in vain;
False magistrates and priests their influence lent
The accursèd thing for lucre to maintain:
Oh fatal thirst of gold! oh foul reproach for Spain!

9.

Oh foul reproach! but not for Spain alone,
But for all lands that bear the Christian name!
Where'er commercial slavery is known,
Oh! shall not Justice, trumpet-tongued, proclaim
The foul reproach, the black offence, the same?
Hear, guilty France! and thou, O England, hear, —
Thou who hast half redeemed thyself from shame!
When slavery from thy realms shall disappear,
Then from this guilt, and not till then, wilt thou be clear.

10.

Unchecked in Paraguay it ran its course,
Till all the gentler children of the land

Well nigh had been consumed without remorse.
The bolder tribes meantime, whose skilful hand
Had tamed the horse, in many a warlike band
Kept the field well with bow and dreadful spear.
And now the Spaniards dared no more withstand
Their force, but in their towns grew pale with fear,
If the Mocobio or the Abipon drew near.

11.

Bear witness, Chaco,—thou, from thy domain
With Spanish blood, as erst with Indian, fed!
And Corrientes, by whose church the slain
Were piled in heaps, till for the gathered dead
One common grave was dug, one service said!
Thou too, Parana, thy sad witness bear
From shores with many a mournful vestige spread,
And monumental crosses here and there,
And monumental names that tell where dwellings were!

12.

Nor would with all their power the Kings of Spain,
Austrian or Bourbon, have at last availed
This torrent of destruction to restrain,
And save a people everywhere assailed
By men before whose face their courage quailed,
But for the virtuous agency of those
Who with the Cross alone, when arms had failed,
Achieved a peaceful triumph o'er the foes,
And gave that weary land the blessings of repose.

13.

For, whensoe'er the Spaniards felt or feared
An Indian enemy, they called for aid
Upon Loyola's sons, now long endeared
To many a happy tribe, by them conveyed
From the open wilderness or woodland shade,
In towns of happiest polity to dwell.
Freely these faithful ministers essayed
The arduous enterprise, contented well
If with success they sped, or if as martyrs fell.

14.

And now it chanced some traders, who had felled
The trees of precious foliage far and wide
On Empalado's shore, when they beheld
The inviting woodlands on its northern side,
Crossed thither in their quest, and there espied
Yeruti's footsteps: searching then the shade,
At length a lonely dwelling they descried,
And, at the thought of hostile hordes dismayed,
To the nearest mission sped, and asked the Jesuit's
aid.

15.

That was a call which ne'er was made in vain
Upon Loyola's sons. In Paraguay,
Much of injustice had they to complain,
Much of neglect; but, faithful laborers they
In the Lord's vineyard, there was no delay
When summoned to his work. A little band

Of converts made them ready for the way;
Their spiritual father took a Cross in hand
To be his staff, and forth they went to search the land.

16.

He was a man of rarest qualities,
Who to this barbarous region had confined
A spirit with the learnèd and the wise
Worthy to take its place, and from mankind
Receive their homage, to the immortal mind
Paid in its just inheritance of fame.
But he to humbler thoughts his heart inclined:
From Gratz, amid the Styrian hills, he came,
And Dobrizhoffer was the good man's honored name.

17.

It was his evil fortune to behold
The labors of his painful life destroyed;
His flock, which he had brought within the fold,
Dispersed; the work of ages rendered void;
And all of good that Paraguay enjoyed
By blind and suicidal Power o'erthrown.
So he the years of his old age employed,
A faithful chronicler, in handing down
Names which he loved, and things well worthy to be known.

18.

And thus, when exiled from the dear-loved scene,
In proud Vienna he beguiled the pain

Of sad remembrance; and the Empress Queen,
That great Teresa, she did not disdain
In gracious mood sometimes to entertain
Discourse with him both pleasurable and sage.
And sure a willing ear she well might deign
To one whose tales may equally engage
The wondering mind of youth, the thoughtful heart of age.

19.

But of his native speech because well nigh
Disuse in him forgetfulness had wrought,
In Latin he composed his history, —
A garrulous, but a lively tale, and fraught
With matter of delight, and food for thought.
And, if he could in Merlin's glass have seen
By whom his tomes to speak our tongue were taught,
The old man would have felt as pleased, I ween,
As when he won the ear of that great Empress Queen.

20.

Little he deemed when with his Indian band
He through the wilds set forth upon his way,
A Poet then unborn, and in a land
Which had proscribed his order, should one day
Take up from thence his moralizing lay,
And shape a song, that, with no fiction dressed,
Should to his worth its grateful tribute pay,
And, sinking deep in many an English breast,
Foster that faith divine that keeps the heart at rest.

21.

Behold him on his way! the breviary,
Which from his girdle hangs, his only shield;
That well-known habit is his panoply;
That Cross, the only weapon he will wield:
By day he bears it for his staff afield,
By night it is the pillow of his bed;
No other lodging these wild woods can yield
Than earth's hard lap, and rustling overhead
A canopy of deep and tangled boughs far spread.

22.

Yet may they not without some cautious care
Take up their inn content upon the ground.
First it behooves to clear a circle there,
And trample down the grass and plantage round,
Where many a deadly reptile might be found,
Whom with its bright and comfortable heat
The flame would else allure: such plagues abound
In these thick woods, and therefore must they beat
The earth, and trample well the herbs beneath their feet.

23.

And now they heap dry reeds and broken wood:
The spark is struck, the crackling fagots blaze,
And cheer that unaccustomed solitude.
Soon have they made their frugal meal of maize;
In grateful adoration then they raise
The evening hymn. How solemn in the wild

That sweet accordant strain wherewith they praise
The Queen of Angels, merciful and mild!
Hail, holiest Mary! Maid, and Mother undefiled.

24.

Blame as thou mayst the Papist's erring creed,
But not their salutary rite of even!
The prayers that from a pious soul proceed,
Though misdirected, reach the ear of Heaven.
Us, unto whom a purer faith is given,
As our best birthright it behooves to hold
The precious charge; but, oh, beware the leaven
Which makes the heart of charity grow cold!
We own one Shepherd, we shall be at last one fold.

25.

Think'st thou the little company, who here
Pour forth their hymn devout at close of day,
Feel it no aid that those who hold them dear,
At the same hour the self-same homage pay,
Commending them to Heaven when far away;
That the sweet bells are heard in solemn chime
Through all the happy towns of Paraguay,
Where now their brethren in one point of time
Join in the general prayer, with sympathy sublime;

26.

That to the glorious Mother of their Lord
Whole Christendom that hour its homage pays;

From court and cottage that with one accord
Ascends the universal strain of praise?
Amid the crowded city's restless ways,
One reverential thought pervades the throng:
The traveller on his lonely road obeys
The sacred hour, and, as he fares along,
In spirit hears and joins his household's even-song.

27.

What if they think that every prayer enrolled
Shall one day in their good account appear;
That guardian Angels hover round, and fold
Their wings in adoration while they hear;
Ministrant Spirits through the ethereal sphere
Waft it with joy, and to the grateful theme,
Well pleased, the Mighty Mother bends her ear?
A vain delusion this we rightly deem:
Yet what they feel is not a mere illusive dream.

28.

That prayer performed, around the fire reclined,
Beneath the leafy canopy they lay
Their limbs: the Indians soon to sleep resigned;
And the good Father with that toilsome day
Fatigued, full fain to sleep, — if sleep he may, —
Whom all-tormenting insects there assail;
More to be dreaded these than beasts of prey
Against whom strength may cope or skill prevail;
But art of man against these enemies must fail.

29.

Patience itself, that should the sovereign cure
For ills that touch ourselves alone, supply,
Lends little aid to one who must endure
This plague: the small tormentors fill the sky,
And swarm about their prey; there he must lie
And suffer while the hours of darkness wear:
At times he utters with a deep-drawn sigh
Some name adored, in accents of despair
Breathed sorrowfully forth, half murmur and half prayer.

30.

Welcome to him the earliest gleam of light;
Welcome to him the earliest sound of day;
That, from the sufferings of that weary night
Released, he may resume his willing way,
Well pleased again the perils to essay
Of that drear wilderness, with hope renewed:
Success will all his labors overpay;
A quest like his is cheerfully pursued;
The heart is happy still that is intent on good.

31.

And now, where Empalado's waters creep
Through low and level shores of woodland wide,
They come: prepared to cross the sluggish deep,
An ill-shaped coracle of hardest hide,
Ruder than ever Cambrian fisher plied
Where Towey and the salt-sea waters meet,

The Indians launch; they steady it and guide,
Winning their way with arms and practised feet,
While in the tottering boat the Father keeps his seat.

32.

For three long summer days, on every side
They search in vain the sylvan solitude;
The fourth a human footstep is espied,
And through the mazes of the pathless wood
With hound-like skill and hawk-like eye pursued;
For keen upon their pious quest are they
As e'er were hunters on the track of blood.
Where softer ground or trodden herbs betray
The slightest mark of man, they there explore the way.

33.

More cautious when more certain of the trace,
In silence they proceed; not like a crew
Of jovial hunters, who the joyous chase
With hound and horn in open field pursue,
Cheering their way with jubilant halloo,
And hurrying forward to their spoil desired,
The panting game before them, full in view:
Humaner thoughts this little band inspired,
Yet with a hope as high their gentle hearts were fired.

34.

Nor is their virtuous hope devoid of fear;
The perils of that enterprise they know:

Some savage horde may have its fastness here,
A race to whom a stranger is a foe,
Who not for friendly words, nor proffered show
Of gifts, will peace or parley entertain.
If by such hands their blameless blood should flow
To serve the Lamb who for their sins was slain,
Blessèd indeed their lot, for so to die is gain!

35.

Them, thus pursuing where the track may lead,
A human voice arrests upon their way:
They stop, and thither, whence the sounds proceed,
All eyes are turned in wonder, — not dismay;
For sure such sounds might charm all fear away:
No nightingale whose brooding mate is nigh,
From some sequestered bower at close of day,
No lark rejoicing in the orient sky,
Ever poured forth so wild a strain of melody.

36.

The voice which through the ringing forest floats
Is one which, having ne'er been taught the skill
Of marshalling sweet words to sweeter notes,
Utters all unpremeditate, at will,
A modulated sequence, loud and shrill,
Of inarticulate and long-breathed sound,
Varying its tones with rise and fall and trill,
Till all the solitary woods around
With that far-piercing power of melody resound.

37.

In mute astonishment attent to hear,
As if by some enchantment held, they stood,
With bending head, fixed eye, and eager ear,
And hand upraised in warning attitude
To check all speech or step that might intrude
On that sweet strain. Them leaving thus spell-bound,
A little way alone into the wood
The Father gently moved toward the sound,
Treading with quiet feet upon the grassy ground.

38.

Anon, advancing thus the trees between,
He saw beside her bower the songstress wild,
Not distant far, himself the while unseen.
Mooma it was, that happy maiden mild,
Who in the sunshine, like a careless child
Of nature, in her joy was carolling.
A heavier heart than his it had beguiled
So to have heard so fair a creature sing
The strains which she had learnt from all sweet birds of spring.

39.

For these had been her teachers, these alone;
And she, in many an emulous essáy,
At length into a descant of her own
Had blended all their notes, — a wild display
Of sounds, in rich, irregular array, —
And now, as blithe as bird in vernal bower,

Poured in full flow the unexpressive lay;
Rejoicing in her consciousness of power,
But in the inborn sense of harmony yet more.

40.

In joy had she begun the ambitious song,
With rapid interchange of sink and swell;
And sometimes high the note was raised, and long
Produced, with shake and effort sensible,
As if the voice exulted there to dwell:
But, when she could no more that pitch sustain,
So thrillingly attuned the cadence fell,
That, with the music of its dying strain,
She moved herself to tears of pleasurable pain.

41.

It might be deemed some dim preságe possessed
The virgin's soul; that some mysterious sense
Of change to come, upon her mind impressed,
Had then called forth, e'er she departed thence,
A requiem to their days of innocence.
For what thou losest in thy native shade
There is one change alone that may compense,
O Mooma! innocent and simple maid, —
Only one change, and it will not be long delayed!

42.

When now the Father issued from the wood
Into that little glade in open sight,

Like one entranced, beholding him, she stood:
Yet had she more of wonder than affright,
Yet less of wonder than of dread delight,
When thus the actual vision came in view;
For instantly the Maiden read aright
Wherefore he came, — his garb and beard she knew.
All that her mother heard had then indeed been true.

43.

Nor was the Father filled with less surprise:
He, too, strange fancies well might entertain,
When this so fair a creature met his eyes.
He might have thought her not of mortal strain;
Rather, as bards of yore were wont to feign,
A nymph divine of Mondai's secret stream;
Or haply of Diana's woodland train:
For, in her beauty, Mooma such might seem,
Being less a child of earth than like a poet's dream.

44.

No art of barbarous ornament had scarred
And stained her virgin limbs, or 'filed her face;
Nor ever yet had evil passion marred
In her sweet countenance the natural grace
Of innocence and youth; nor was there trace
Of sorrow, or of hardening want and care.
Strange was it in this wild and savage place,
Which seemed to be for beasts a fitting lair,
Thus to behold a maid so gentle and so fair.

45.

Across her shoulders was a hammock flung:
By night it was the Maiden's bed; by day,
Her only garment. Round her as it hung,
In short, unequal folds of loose array,
The open meshes, when she moves, display
Her form. She stood with fixed and wondering
eyes;
And trembling like a leaf upon the spray,
Even for excess of joy, with eager cries
She called her mother forth to share that glad
surprise.

46.

At that unwonted call, with quickened pace,
The Matron hurried thither, half in fear.
How strange to Monnema a stranger's face!
How strange it was a stranger's voice to hear!
How strangely to her disaccustomed ear
Came even the accents of her native tongue!
But, when she saw her countrymen appear,
Tears for that unexpected blessing sprung,
And once again she felt as if her heart were young.

47.

Soon was her melancholy story told;
And glad consent unto that Father good
Was given, that they to join his happy fold
Would leave with him their forest solitude.
Why comes not now Yeruti from the wood?
Why tarrieth he so late this blessèd day?

They long to see their joy in his renewed,
And look impatiently toward his way,
And think they hear his step, and chide his long delay.

48.

He comes at length, a happy man, to find
His only dream of hope fulfilled at last.
The sunshine of his all-believing mind
There is no doubt or fear to overcast;
No chilling forethought checks his bliss; the past
Leaves no regret for him; and all to come
Is change and wonder and delight. How fast
Hath busy fancy conjured up a sum
Of joys unknown, whereof the expectance makes him dumb!

49.

Oh happy day! the Messenger of Heaven
Hath found them in their lonely dwelling-place!
Oh happy day! to them it would be given
To share in that Eternal Mother's grace,
And one day see in heaven her glorious face,
Where Angels round her mercy-throne adore!
Now shall they mingle with the human race,
Sequestered from their fellow-kind no more:
Oh joy of joys supreme! oh bliss for them in store!

50.

Full of such hopes this night they lay them down,
But not, as they were wont, this night to rest.

Their old tranquillity of heart is gone;
The peace wherewith till now they have been blest
Hath taken its departure. In the breast
Fast-following thoughts and busy fancies throng;
Their sleep itself is feverish, and possessed
With dreams that to the wakeful mind belong:
To Mooma and the youth then first the night seemed
long.

51.

Day comes; and now a first and last farewell
To that fair bower within their native wood,
Their quiet nest till now. The bird may dwell
Henceforth in safety there, and rear her brood,
And beasts and reptiles undisturbed intrude:
Reckless of this, the simple tenants go,
Emerging from their peaceful solitude,
To mingle with the world, but not to know
Its crimes, nor to partake its cares, nor feel its woe.

CANTO IV.

1.

The bells rung blithely from St. Mary's tower,
When in St. Joachin's the news was told
That Dobrizhoffer from his quest that hour
Drew nigh: the glad Guaranies, young and old,
Throng through the gate, rejoicing to behold
His face again; and all with heartfelt glee

Welcome the Pastor to his peaceful fold,
Where so beloved amid his flock was he,
That this return was like a day of jubilee.

2.

How more than strange, how marvellous a sight,
To the new-comers was this multitude!
Something like fear was mingled with affright,
When they the busy scene of turmoil viewed:
Wonder itself the sense of joy subdued,
And, with its all-unwonted weight, oppressed
These children of the quiet solitude;
And now and then a sigh, that heaved the breast
Unconsciously, bewrayed their feeling of unrest.

3.

Not more prodigious than that little town
Seemed to these comers were the pomp and power
To us of ancient Rome in her renown;
Nor the elder Babylon, or ere that hour
When her high gardens, and her cloud-capt tower,
And her broad walls, before the Persian fell;
Nor those dread fanes on Nile's forsaken shore,
Whose ruins yet their pristine grandeur tell,
Wherein the demon Gods themselves might deign
to dwell.

4.

But if, all humble as it was, that scene
Possessed a poor and uninstructed mind

With awe, the thoughtful spirit, well I ween,
Something to move its wonder there might find,
Something of consolation for its kind,
Some hope and earnest of a happier age,
When vain pursuits no more the heart shall blind,
But Faith the evils of this earth assuage,
And to all souls assure their heavenly heritage.

5.

Yes; for, in history's mournful map, the eye
On Paraguay, as on a sunny spot,
May rest complacent: to humanity,
There, and there only, hath a peaceful lot
Been granted, by Ambition troubled not,
By Avarice undebased, exempt from care,
By perilous passions undisturbed. And what
If Glory never reared her standard there,
Nor with her clarion's blast awoke the slumbering air?—

6.

Content and cheerful Piety were found
Within those humble walls. From youth to age
The simple dwellers paced their even round
Of duty, not desiring to engage
Upon the busy world's contentious stage,
Whose ways they wisely had been trained to dread:
Their inoffensive lives in pupilage
Perpetually, but peacefully, they led,
From all temptation saved, and sure of daily bread.

7.

They on the Jesuit, who was nothing loath,
Reposed alike their conscience and their cares;
And he, with equal faith, the trust of both
Accepted and discharged. The bliss is theirs
Of that entire dependence that prepares
Entire submission, let what may befall;
And his whole careful course of life declares
That for their good he holds them thus in thrall,
Their Father and their Friend, Priest, Ruler, all in all.

8.

Food, raiment, shelter, safety, he provides;
No forecast, no anxieties, have they;
The Jesuit governs and instructs and guides;
Their part it is to honor and obey,
Like children under wise parental sway.
All thoughts and wishes are to him confessed;
And when, at length, in life's last, weary day,
In sure and certain hope they sink to rest,
By him their eyes are closed, by him their burial blest.

9.

Deem not their lives of happiness devoid,
Though thus the years their course obscurely fill;
In rural and in household arts employed,
And many a pleasing task of pliant skill,
For emulation here unmixed with ill,
Sufficient scope was given. Each had assigned

His proper part, which yet left free the will;
So well they knew to mould the ductile mind
By whom the scheme of that wise order was combined.

10.

It was a land of priestcraft, but the Priest
Believed himself the fables that he taught:
Corrupt their forms, and yet those forms at least
Preserved a salutary faith that wrought,
Maugre the alloy, the saving end it sought.
Benevolence had gained such empire there,
That even superstition had been brought
An aspect of humanity to wear,
And make the weal of man its first and only care.

11.

Nor lacked they store of innocent delight,
Music and song and dance and proud array,
Whate'er might win the ear or charm the sight;
Banners and pageantry in rich display
Brought forth upon some Saint's high holyday,
The altar dressed, the church with garlands hung,
Arches and floral bowers beside the way,
And festal tables spread for old and young,
Gladness in every heart, and mirth on every tongue.

12.

Thou who despisest so debased a fate,
As in the pride of wisdom thou mayst call

These meek, submissive Indians' low estate,
Look round the world, and see where over all
Injurious passions hold mankind in thrall;
How barbarous Force asserts a ruthless reign;
Or Mammon, o'er his portion of the ball,
Hath learned a baser empire to maintain, —
Mammon, the god of all who give their souls to gain.

13.

Behold the fraudful arts, the covert strife,
The jarring interests, that engross mankind;
The low pursuits, the selfish aims of life;
Studies that weary and contract the mind, —
That bring no joy, and leave no peace behind;
And Death approaching to dissolve the spell!
The immortal soul, which hath so long been blind,
Recovers then clear sight, and sees too well
The error of its ways, when irretrievable.

14.

Far happier the Guaranies' humble race,
With whom, in dutiful contentment wise,
The gentle virtues had their dwelling-place.
With them the dear, domestic charities
Sustained no blight from fortune; natural ties
There suffered no divorcement, save alone
That which in course of nature might arise;
No artificial wants and ills were known;
But there they dwelt as if the world were all their own.

15.

Obedience in its laws that takes delight
Was theirs; simplicity that knows no art;
Love, friendship, grateful duty, in its height;
Meekness and truth, that keep all strife apart;
And faith and hope, which elevate the heart
Upon its heavenly heritage intent.
Poor, erring, self-tormentor that thou art,
O Man! and on thine own undoing bent,
Wherewith canst thou be blest, if not with these content?

16.

Mild pupils in Submission's perfect school,
Two thousand souls were gathered here; and here,
Beneath the Jesuit's all-embracing rule,
They dwelt, obeying him with love sincere,
That never knew distrust, nor felt a fear,
Nor anxious thought, which wears the heart away.
Sacred to them their laws, their Ruler dear;
Humbler or happier none could be than they,
Who knew it for their good in all things to obey.

17.

The Patron Saint, from whom their town was named,
Was that St. Joachin, who, legends say,
Unto the Saints in Limbo first proclaimed
The Advent. Being permitted, on the day
That Death enlarged him from this mortal clay,
His daughter's high election to behold,

Thither his soul, glad herald, winged its way,
And to the Prophets and the Patriarchs old
The tidings of great joy and near deliverance told.

18.

There on the altar was his image set,
The lamp before it burning night and day,
And there was incensed, when his votaries met
Before the sacred shrine their beads to say,
And for his fancied intercession pray,
Devoutly as in faith they bent the knee.
Such adoration they were taught to pay:
Good man, how little had he weened that he
Should thus obtain a place in Rome's idolatry!

19.

But chiefly there the Mother of our Lord,
His blessèd daughter, by the multitude
Was for their special patroness adored.
Amid the square on high her image stood,
Clasping the Babe in her beatitude,—
The Babe Divine, on whom she fixed her sight;
And in their hearts, albe the work was rude,
It raised the thought of all-commanding might,
Combined with boundless love and mercy infinite.

20.

To this great family the Jesuit brought
His new-found children now; for young and old

He deemed alike his children while he wrought
For their salvation, — seeking to unfold
The saving mysteries in the creed enrolled,
To their slow minds, that could but ill conceive
The import of the mighty truths he told.
But errors they have none to which they cleave;
And whatsoe'er he tells they willingly believe.

21.

Safe from that pride of ignorance were they
That with small knowledge thinks itself full wise.
How at believing aught should these delay,
When everywhere new objects met their eyes
To fill the soul with wonder and surprise?
Not of itself, but by temptation bred,
In man doth impious unbelief arise;
It is our instinct to believe and dread:
God bids us love, and then our faith is perfected.

22.

Quick to believe, and slow to comprehend,
Like children, unto all the teacher taught
Submissively an easy ear they lend.
And to the font at once he might have brought
These converts, if the Father had not thought
Theirs was a case for wise and safe delay,
Lest lightly learnt might lightly be forgot;
And meanwhile due instruction day by day
Would to their opening minds the sense of truth convey.

23.

Of this they recked not whether soon or late;
For overpowering wonderment possessed
Their faculties; and in this new estate
Strange sights and sounds and thoughts well nigh oppressed
Their sense, and raised a turmoil in the breast,
Resenting less of pleasure than of pain;
And sleep afforded them no natural rest,
But in their dreams, a mixed, disordered train,
The busy scenes of day disturbed their hearts again.

24.

Even when the spirit to that secret wood
Returned, slow Mondai's silent stream beside,
No longer there it found the solitude
Which late it left: strange faces were descried,
Voices, and sounds of music far and wide,
And buildings seemed to tower amid the trees,
And forms of men and beasts on every side,
As ever-wakeful fancy hears and sees
All things that it had heard and seen, and more than these.

25.

For in their sleep strange forms deformed they saw
Of frightful fiends, their ghostly enemies,
And souls who must abide the rigorous law
Weltering in fire, and there with dolorous cries

Blaspheming roll around their hopeless eyes;
And those who, doomed a shorter term to bear
In penal flames, look upward to the skies,
Seeking and finding consolation there,
And feel, like dew from heaven, the precious aid of prayer.

26.

And Angels who around their glorious Queen
In adoration bent their heads abased;
And infant faces in their dreams were seen
Hovering on cherub-wings; and Spirits placed
To be their guards invisible, who chased
With fiery arms their fiendish foes away:
Such visions overheated fancy traced,
Peopling the night with a confused array
That made its hours of rest more restless than the day.

27.

To all who, from an old erratic course
Of life, within the Jesuit's fold were led,
The change was perilous. They felt the force
Of habit, when, till then in forests bred,
A thick, perpetual umbrage overhead,
They came to dwell in open light and air.
This ill the Fathers long had learnt to dread,
And still devised such means as might prepare
The new-reclaimed unhurt this total change to bear.

28.

All thoughts and occupations to commute,
To change their air, their water, and their food,
And those old habits suddenly uproot,
Conformed to which the vital powers pursued
Their functions, — such mutation is too rude
For man's fine frame unshaken to sustain.
And these poor children of the solitude
Began ere long to pay the bitter pain
That their new way of life brought with it in its
train.

29.

On Monnema the apprehended ill
Came first: the Matron sunk beneath the weight
Of a strong malady, whose force no skill
In healing might avert or mitigate.
Yet, happy in her children's safe estate,
Her thankfulness for them she still expressed;
And, yielding then complacently to fate,
With Christian rites her passing hour was blest,
And with a Christian's hope she was consigned to
rest.

30.

They laid her in the Garden of the Dead:
Such as a Christian burial-place should be
Was that fair spot, where every grave was spread
With flowers, and not a weed to spring was
free;
But the pure blossoms of the orange-tree
Dropped like a shower of fragrance on the bier;

And palms, the type of immortality,
Planted in stately colonnades appear,
That all was verdant there throughout the unvarying year.

31.

Nor ever did irreverent feet intrude
Within that sacred spot; nor sound of mirth,
Unseemly there, profane the solitude,
Where solemnly committed earth to earth,
Waiting the summons for their second birth,
Whole generations in Death's peaceful fold
Collected lay, — green innocence, ripe worth,
Youth full of hope, and age whose days were told,
Compressed alike into that mass of mortal mould.

32.

Mortal, and yet at the Archangel's voice
To put on immortality. That call
Shall one day make the sentient dust rejoice;
These bodies then shall rise, and cast off all
Corruption, with whate'er of earthly thrall
Had clogged the heavenly image then set free.
How, then, should death a Christian's heart appall?
Lo, Heaven for you is open! enter, ye
Children of God, and heirs of his eternity!

33.

This hope supported Mooma, hand in hand
When with Yeruti at the grave she stood.

Less even now of death they understand
Than of the joys eternal that ensued:
The bliss of infinite beatitude
To them had been their teacher's favorite theme,
Wherewith their hearts so fully were imbued,
That it the sole reality might seem,
Life, death, and all things else, a shadow or a dream.

34.

Yea, so possessed with that best hope were they,
That if the heavens had opened overhead,
And the Archangel with his trump that day
To judgment had convoked the quick and dead,
They would have heard the summons, not with dread,
But in the joy of faith that knows no fear:
"Come, Lord! come quickly!" would this pair have said;
"And thou, O Queen of men and Angels dear!
Lift us, whom thou hast loved, into thy happy sphere."

35.

They wept not at the grave, though overwrought
With feelings there as if the heart would break.
Some haply might have deemed they suffered not,
Yet they who looked upon that Maiden meek
Might see what deep emotion blanched her cheek.
An inward light there was which filled her eyes,
And told, more forcibly than words could speak,
That this disruption of her earliest ties
Had shaken mind and frame in all their faculties.

36.

It was not passion only that disturbed
Her gentle nature thus; it was not grief;
Nor human feeling by the effort curbed
Of some misdeeming duty, when relief
Were surely to be found, albeit brief,
If sorrow at its springs might freely flow;
Nor yet repining, stronger than belief
In its first force, that shook the Maiden so;
Though these alone might that frail fabric overthrow.

37.

The seeds of death were in her at that hour;
Soon was their quickening and their growth displayed:
Thenceforth she drooped and withered like a flower,
Which, when it flourished in its native shade,
Some child to his own garden hath conveyed,
And planted in the sun, to pine away.
Thus was the gentle Mooma seen to fade,
Not under sharp disease, but day by day
Losing the powers of life in visible decay.

38.

The sunny hue that tinged her cheek was gone;
A deathy paleness settled in its stead;
The light of joy which in her eyes had shone,
Now, like a lamp that is no longer fed,
Grew dim: but when she raised her heavy head,
Some proffered help of kindness to partake,

Those feeble eyes a languid lustre shed,
And her sad smile of thankfulness would wake
Grief even in callous hearts for that sweet sufferer's
sake.

39.

How had Yeruti borne to see her fade?
But he was spared the lamentable sight,
Himself upon the bed of sickness laid.
Joy of his heart, and of his eyes the light,
Had Mooma been to him, his soul's delight,
On whom his mind for ever was intent;
His darling thought by day, his dream by night,
The playmate of his youth in mercy sent,
With whom his life had passed in peacefulest content.

40.

Well was it for the youth, and well for her,
As there in placid helplessness she lay,
He was not present with his love to stir
Emotions that might shake her feeble clay,
And rouse up in her heart a strong array
Of feelings, hurtful only when they bind
To earth the soul that soon must pass away.
But this was spared them; and no pain of mind
To trouble her had she, instinctively resigned.

41.

Nor was there wanting to the sufferers aught
Of careful kindness to alleviate

The affliction; for the universal thought
In that poor town was of their sad estate,
And what might best relieve or mitigate
Their case, what help of nature or of art;
And many were the prayers compassionate
That the good Saints their healing would impart,
Breathed in that Maid's behalf from many a tender heart.

42.

And vows were made for her, if vows might save:
She for herself the while preferred no prayer;
For, when she stood beside her Mother's grave,
Her earthly hopes and thoughts had ended there.
Her only longing now was, free as air
From this obstructive flesh to take her flight
For Paradise, and seek her Mother there;
And then, regaining her belovèd sight,
Rest in the eternal sense of undisturbed delight.

43.

Her heart was there; and there she felt and knew
That soon full surely should her spirit be.
And who can tell what foretastes might ensue
To one whose soul, from all earth's thraldom free,
Was waiting thus for immortality?
Sometimes she spake with short and hurried breath,
As if some happy sight she seemed to see,
While, in the fulness of a perfect faith,
Even with a lover's hope, she lay, and looked for death.

44.

I said that for herself the patient Maid
Preferred no prayer: but oft her feeble tongue
And feebler breath a voice of praise essayed;
And, duly when the vesper-bell was rung,
Her evening hymn in faint accord she sung,
So piously, that they who gathered round,
Awe-stricken on her heavenly accents hung,
As though they thought it were no mortal sound,
But that the place whereon they stood was holy ground.

45.

At such an hour, when Dobrizhoffer stood
Beside her bed, oh! how unlike, he thought,
This voice to that which, ringing through the wood,
Had led him to the secret bower he sought!
And was it then for this that he had brought
That harmless household from their native shade?
Death had already been the Mother's lot;
And this fair Mooma, was she formed to fade
So soon, — so soon must she in earth's cold lap be laid?

46.

Yet he had no misgiving at the sight;
And wherefore should he? He had acted well;
And, deeming of the ways of God aright,
Knew that to such as these, whate'er befell
Must needs for them be best. But who could dwell
Unmoved upon the fate of one so young,

So blithesome late? What marvel if tears fell
From that good man as over her he hung,
And that the prayers he said came faltering from
his tongue?

47.

She saw him weep; and she could understand
The cause thus tremulously that made him speak.
By his emotion moved, she took his hand:
A gleam of pleasure o'er her pallid cheek
Passed, while she looked at him with meaning
And for a little while, as loath to part, [meek,
Detaining him, her fingers, lank and weak,
Played with their hold; then, letting him depart,
She gave him a slow smile that touched him to the
heart.

48.

Mourn not for her! for what hath life to give
That should detain her ready spirit here?
Think'st thou that it were worth a wish to live,
Could wishes hold her from her proper sphere?
That simple heart, that innocence sincere,
The world would stain. Fitter she ne'er could be
For the great change; and, now that change is
near,
Oh! who would keep her soul from being free?
Maiden beloved of Heaven, to die is best for thee!

49.

She hath passed away; and on her lips a smile
Hath settled, fixed in death. Judged they aright,

Or suffered they their fancy to beguile
The reason, who believed that she had sight
Of Heaven before her spirit took its flight;
That Angels waited round her lowly bed;
And that, in that last effort of delight,
When lifting up her dying arms, she said,
"I come!" a ray from heaven upon her face was shed?

50.

St. Joachin's had never seen a day
Of such profuse and general grief before,
As when, with tapers, dirge, and long array,
The Maiden's body to the grave they bore.
All eyes, all hearts, her early death deplore;
Yet, wondering at the fortune they lament,
They the wise ways of Providence adore,
By whom the Pastor surely had been sent,
When to the Mondai woods upon his quest he went.

51.

This was, indeed, a chosen family,
For Heaven's especial favor marked, they said;
Shut out from all mankind they seemed to be;
Yet mercifully they were visited,
That so within the fold they might be led,
Then called away to bliss. Already two
In their baptismal innocence were dead;
The third was on the bed of death, they knew,
And in the appointed course must presently ensue.

52.

They marvelled, therefore, when the youth once more
Rose from his bed, and walked abroad again:
Severe had been the malady, and sore
The trial, while life struggled to maintain
Its seat against the sharp assaults of pain.
But life in him was vigorous; long he lay
Ere it could its ascendency regain;
Then, when the natural powers resumed their sway,
All trace of late disease passed rapidly away.

53.

The first inquiry, when his mind was free,
Was for his Sister. She was gone, they said, —
Gone to her Mother, evermore to be
With her in Heaven. At this no tears he shed,
Nor was he seen to sorrow for the dead;
But took the fatal tidings in such part
As if a dull, unfeeling nature bred
His unconcern; for hard would seem the heart
To which a loss like his no suffering could impart.

54.

How little do they see what is, who frame
Their hasty judgment upon that which seems!
Waters that babble on their way proclaim
A shallowness; but in their strength deep streams
Flow silently. Of death, Yeruti deems
Not as an ill, but as the last great good,

Compared wherewith all other he esteems
Transient and void: how, then, should thought
intrude
Of sorrow in his heart for their beatitude?

55.

While dwelling in their sylvan solitude,
Less had Yeruti learnt to entertain
A sense of age than death. He understood
Something of death from creatures he had slain;
But here the ills which follow in the train
Of age had first to him been manifest, —
The shrunken form, the limbs that move with pain,
The failing sense, infirmity, unrest, —
That in his heart he said to die betimes was best.

56.

Nor had he lost the dead: they were but gone
Before him, whither he should shortly go.
Their robes of glory they had first put on:
He, cumbered with mortality, below
Must yet abide awhile, content to know
He should not wait in long expectance here.
What cause, then, for repining or for woe?
Soon shall he join them in their heavenly sphere;
And often, even now, he knew that they were near.

57.

'Twas but in open day to close his eyes,
And shut out the unprofitable view

Of all this weary world's realities,
And forthwith, even as if they lived anew,
The dead were with him; features, form, and hue,
And looks and gestures, were restored again:
Their actual presence in his heart he knew;
And when their converse was disturbed, oh! then
How flat and stale it was to mix with living men!

58.

But not the less, whate'er was to be done,
With living men he took his part content,
At loom, in garden, or afield, as one
Whose spirit, wholly on obedience bent,
To every task its prompt attention lent.
Alert in labor he among the best;
And, when to church the congregation went,
None more exact than he to cross his breast,
And kneel or rise, and do in all things like the rest.

59.

Cheerful he was, almost like one elate
With wine, before it hath disturbed his power
Of reason. Yet he seemed to feel the weight
Of time; for always, when from yonder tower
He heard the clock tell out the passing hour,
The sound appeared to give him some delight;
And, when the evening shades began to lower,
Then was he seen to watch the fading light,
As if his heart rejoiced at the return of night.

60.

The old man, to whom he had been given in care,
To Dobrizhoffer came one day, and said,
"The trouble which our youth was thought to bear
With such indifference hath deranged his head.
He says that he is nightly visited;
His Mother and his Sister come and say
That he must give this message from the dead, —
Not to defer his baptism, and delay
A soul upon the earth which should no longer stay."

61.

A dream the Jesuit deemed it; a deceit,
Upon itself by feverish fancy wrought;
A mere delusion, which it were not meet
To censure, lest the youth's distempered thought
Might thereby be to further error brought:
But he himself its vanity would find, —
They argued thus, — if it were noticed not.
His baptism was in fitting time designed,
The Father said, and then dismissed it from his mind.

62.

But the old Indian came again ere long
With the same tale, and freely then confessed
His doubt that he had done Yeruti wrong;
For something more than common seemed impressed.
And now he thought that certes it were best
From the youth's lips his own account to hear;

Haply the Father then to his request
Might yield, regarding his desire sincere,
Nor wait for further time if there were aught to fear.

63.

Considerately the Jesuit heard, and bade
The Youth be called. Yeruti told his tale.
Nightly these blessèd spirits came, he said,
To warn him he must come within the pale
Of Christ without delay; nor must he fail
This warning to their Pastor to repeat,
Till the renewed entreaty should prevail:
Life's business then for him would be complete,
And 'twas to tell him this they left their starry seat.

64.

Came they to him in dreams? — he could not tell;
Sleeping or waking now small difference made:
For even, while he slept, he knew full well
That his dear Mother and that darling Maid
Both in the Garden of the Dead were laid.
And yet he saw them as in life, the same,
Save only that in radiant robes arrayed;
And round about their presence, when they came,
There shone an effluent light as of a harmless flame.

65.

And where he was he knew, the time, the place, —
All circumstantial things to him were clear,

His own heart undisturbed. His Mother's face
How could he choose but know; or, knowing, fear
Her presence and that Maid's, to him more dear
Than all that had been left him now below?
Their love had drawn them from their happy sphere;
That dearest love unchanged they came to show;
And he must be baptized, and then he, too, might go.

66.

With searching ken, the Jesuit, while he spake,
Perused him, if in countenance or tone
Aught might be found appearing to partake
Of madness. Mark of passion there was none;
None of derangement: in his eye alone,
As from a hidden fountain emanate,
Something of an unusual brightness shone:
But neither word nor look betrayed a state
Of wandering; and his speech, though earnest, was sedate.

67.

Regular his pulse, from all disorder free;
The vital powers performed their part assigned;
And, to whate'er was asked, collectedly
He answered. Nothing troubled him in mind:
Why should it? Were not all around him kind?
Did not all love him with a love sincere,
And seem, in serving him, a joy to find?

He had no want, no pain, no grief, no fear:
But he must be baptized; he could not tarry here.

68.

"Thy will be done, Father in heaven who art!"
The Pastor said, nor longer now denied;
But, with a weight of awe upon his heart,
Entered the church; and there, the font beside,
With holy water, chrism, and salt applied,
Performed in all solemnity the rite.
His feeling was that hour with fear allied:
Yeruti's was a sense of pure delight;
And, while he knelt, his eyes seemed larger and more bright.

69.

His wish hath been obtained; and, this being done,
His soul was to its full desire content.
The day in its accustomed course passed on;
The Indian marked him ere to rest he went,
How o'er his beads, as he was wont, he bent,
And then, like one who casts all care aside,
Lay down. The old man feared no ill event,
When, "Ye are come for me!" Yeruti cried:
"Yes, I am ready now!" and instantly he died.

NOTES TO A TALE OF PARAGUAY.

So he, forsooth, a shapely boot must wear. — Proem, p. 10.

His leg had been set by the French after their conquest of Pamplona, and reset after his removal to his father's house. The latter operation is described as having been most severe, but borne by him, in his wonted manner, without any manifestation of suffering. For some time, his life was despaired of. "When the danger of death was past, and the bones were knit and becoming firm, two inconveniences remained: one occasioned by a portion of bone below the knee, which projected so as to occasion some deformity; the other was a contraction of the leg, which prevented him from walking erect, or standing firmly on his feet. Now, as he was very solicitous about his appearance, and intended at that time to follow the course of a military life, which he had begun, he inquired of his medical attendants, in the first place, whether the bone could be removed, which stood out in so unsightly a manner. They answered, that it was possible to remove it, but the operation would be exceedingly painful, — much more so than any which he had before undergone. He nevertheless directed them to cut it out, that he might have his will, and (as he himself related in my hearing, says Ribadeneira) that he might wear fashionable and well-fitting boots. Nor could he be dissuaded from this determination. He would not consent to be bound during the operation, and went through it with the same firmness of mind which he had manifested in the former operations. By this means, the deformity of the bone was removed. The contraction of the leg was in some degree relieved by other applications, and especially by certain machines, with which during many days, and with great and continual pain, it was stretched: nevertheless, it could not be so extended but that it always remained something shorter than the other." — *Ribadeneira, Vita S. Ignatii Loyolæ, Acta SS. Jul.*, t. vii. p. 659.

A close-fitting boot seems to have been as fashionable at one time as close-fitting *innominables* of buckskin were about the year 1790; and perhaps it was as severe an operation to get into them for the first time. "The greasy shoemaker," says Tom Nash, "with his squirrel's-skin, and a whole stall of ware upon his arm, enters, and wrencheth his legs for an hour together, and after shows his tally. By St. Loy, that draws deep!" — *Nash's Lenten Stuff. Harl. Miscel.*, vol. ii. p. 289, 8vo edition.

The operation of fitting a Spanish dandy with short-laced quarter boots is thus minutely described by Juan de Zavaleta, who was historiographer at the commencement of Carlos II.'s reign: —

"In comes the shoemaker in the odor of haste and fatigue: he takes the shoes off the last with as much difficulty as if he were skinning the lasts. The gallant seats himself upon a chair: the shoemaker kneels down, and takes possession of one foot, which he handles as if he were sent there to administer the torture. He puts one shoeing-skin* in the heel of the shoe, fits the other upon the point of the foot, and then begins to guide the shoe over the shoeing-skin. Scarcely has it got farther than the toes when it is found necessary to draw it on with pincers; and even then it is hard work. The patient stands up, fatigued with the operation, but well pleased that the shoes are tight; and, by the shoemaker's directions, he stamps three or four times on the floor with such force, that it must be of iron if it does not give way.

"The cordovan and the soles, being thus beaten, submit: they are the skins of animals who obey blows. Our gallant returns to his seat: he turns up the upper leather of the shoe, and lays hold on it with the pincers. The tradesman kneels

* A piece of hare's-skin is used in Spain for this purpose, as it appears by the former extract from Tom Nash that squirrel's-skin was in England.

close by him on both knees; rests on the ground with his left hand; and bending in this all-four's position over the foot, making an arch with those fingers of the right hand which form the span, assists in drawing on the upper part of the cordovan; the gallant pulling the while with the pincers. He then puts himself on one knee, lays hold of the end of the foot with one hand, and with the palm of the other strikes his own hand as hard as if he were striking a ball with a racket; for necessity is so discreet, that the poor man inflicts this pain upon himself that he may give none to the person of whose custom he stands in need.

"The end of the foot being thus adjusted, he repairs to the heel, and with his tongue moistens the end of the seams, that they may not give way for being dry. Tremendous vanity, that one man should allow the mouth of another to be applied to his feet that he may have them trimly set out! The shoemaker unfolds the heel, turns round with the shoeing-skin in his hand, and begins to fit the second part of the shoe upon the foot. He desires the gallant to put the end of the foot down; and the gallant does as he is desired. He draws the shoe towards him with such force, that the person who is thus being shoed is compressed in an unseemly manner between the shoemaker's body and the back of the chair. Presently he tells him to put his heel down; and the man is as obedient as a slave. He orders him then to stamp upon the ground; and the man stamps as he is ordered. The gallant then seats himself again: the cruel operator draws the shoeing-skin from the instep, and in its place drives in a stick which they call *costa.** He then turns upon it the punch, which makes the holes in the leather through which the ribbons are to pass: he again twists round his hand the strip of hare's-skin which hangs from the heel, and pulls it as if he were ringing a bell, and leaves upon the upper part of the top such pain and marks as if he had punched the holes in it. He bores the ears, passes the string through with a bodkin, brings the ears together that they may fasten the shoe, fits them to their in-

* Which is used to drive in upon the last to raise a shoe higher in the instep.

tended place, and ties the knot with such force, that, if it were possible to strangle a man by the neck of his foot, strangled the gallant would be. Then he makes the rose, with more care than grace. He goes then to take out the shoeing-skin, which is still hanging from the heel: he lays hold of this, strikes the sole of the foot with his other hand as if settling it, and draws out the skin, bringing out all with it. The gallant puts his foot to the ground, and remains looking at it: the shoemaker rises, wipes the sweat from his forehead with his fingers, and draws his breath like one who has been running. All this trouble might have been saved by making the shoe a little larger than the foot. Presently both have to go through the same pains with the other foot. Now comes the last and terrible act of payment. The tradesman collects his tools, receives his money, and goes out at the door, looking at the silver to see if it is good, and leaving the gallant walking as much at his ease as if he had been put in fetters.

"If they who wear tight shoes think that thereby they can lessen the size of their feet, they are mistaken: the bones cannot be squeezed one into another. If, therefore, the shoe is made short, the foot must be crooked at the joints, and grow upward if it is not allowed to grow forward; if it is pinched in the breadth, the flesh which is thus constrained must extend itself in length. They who are shod thus miserably remain with just the same quantity of foot.

"Of all animals, man is the one to which, in proportion to its size, Nature has given the largest feet; because as his whole body is to be supported upon them, and he has only two, she chose that he should walk in safety. He who wishes to abbreviate them acts as if he were inclined to fall, and to fall into vices which will do him more injury than if he fell upon stones. The feet are the part which in the fabric of the human body are placed nearest to the earth. They are meant, therefore, to be the humblest part of his frame; but gallants take away all humility by adorning and setting them forth in bravery. This so displeases the Creator, that, having to make man an animal who should walk upon the earth, he made the earth of such properties that the footsteps should sink into it. The foot which is lifted from the ground leaves its own grave open, and seems as if it rose from the grave. What a tremendous thing is it, then, to set off with adornments that which the earth wishes to devour at every step!" — *El dia de Fiesta: Obras de D. Juan de Zavaleta*, pp. 179, 180.

Whiling with books the weary hours away. — Proem, p. 10.

"Vede quanto importa a liçaõ de bons livros! Se o livr fora de cavallerias, sahiria Ignacio hum grande cavalleyro: foy hum livro de Vidas de Santos, sahio hum grande santo. Se lera cavallerias, sahiria Ignacio hum Cavalleyro da Ardente Espada: leo vidas de santos, sahio hum Santo da Ardente Tocha." — *Vieyra: Sermam de S. Ignacio*, t. i. 368.

"See," says Vieyra, "the importance of reading good books! If it had been a book of knight-errantry, Ignacio would have become a great knight-errant: it was the Lives of the Saints, and Ignatius became a great saint. If he had read about knights, he might have proved a Knight of the Burning Sword: he read about saints, and proved a Saint of the Burning Torch."

Nothing could seem more probable than that Cervantes had this part of Loyola's history in his mind when he described the rise of Don Quixote's madness, if Cervantes had not shown himself in one of his dramas to be thoroughly imbued with the pestilent superstition of his country. "El dichoso Rufian" is one of those monstrous compositions which nothing but the antichristian fables of the Romish church could have produced.

Landor, however, supposes that Cervantes intended to satirize a favorite dogma of the Spaniards. The passage occurs in his thirteenth conversation.

"The most dexterous attack ever made against the worship among Catholics, which opens so many side-chapels to pilfering and imposture, is that of Cervantes.

"*Leopold.* I do not remember in what part.

"*President.* Throughout 'Don Quixote.' Dulcinea was the peerless, the immaculate; and death was denounced against all who hesitated to admit the assertion of her perfections. Surely your highness never could have imagined that Cervantes was such a knight-errant as to attack knight-errantry; a folly that had ceased more than a century, if indeed it was any folly at all. And the idea that he ridiculed the poems and romances founded on it is not less improbable; for they contained all the literature of the nation, excepting the garniture of chapter-houses, theology, and pervaded, as with a thread of gold, the beautiful histories of this illustrious people. He delighted the idlers of romance by the jokes he scattered amongst them on the false taste of his predecessors and of his rivals; and he delighted his own heart by this solitary archery, well knowing what amusement those who came another day would find in picking up his arrows and discovering the bull's-eye hits.

"Charles V. was the Knight of La Mancha, devoting his labors and vigils, his wars and treaties, to the chimerical idea of making all minds, like watches, turn their indexes by a simultaneous movement to one point. Sancho Panza was the symbol of the people, possessing sound sense in all other matters, but ready to follow the most extravagant visionary in this, and combining implicit belief in it with the grossest sensuality; for religion, when it is hot enough to produce enthusiasm, burns up and kills every seed intrusted to its bosom." — *Imaginary Conversations*, vol. i. 187.

The Jesuits, however, assure us that Loyola is *not* the author of their society, and that it is not allowable either to think or say so. "Societas Jesu ut à S. Ignatio de Loiolâ non ducit nomen, ita neque originem primam, et aliud sentire aut loqui, nefas." — *Imago Primi Sæculi Soc. Jesu*, p. 64. "Jesus primus ac præcipuus auctor Societatis" is the title of a chapter in this their secular volume, which is a curious and very beautiful book. Then follows "Beata Virgo nutrix, patrona, imò altera velut auctor Societatis." Lastly, "Post Christum et Mariam, Societatis Auctor et Parens sanctus Ignatius."

"On the 26th August, 1794, the French plundered the rich church of Loyola, at Azpeitia, and, proceeding to Elgoibas, loaded five carts with the spoils of the church of that place. This party of marauders consisted of two hundred. The peasants collected, fell upon them, and, after an obstinate conflict of three hours, recovered the whole booty, which they conveyed to

Vittoria in triumph. Among other things, a relic of Loyola was recovered, which was carried in procession to the church, the victorious peasants accompanying it." — *Marcillac, Hist. de la Guerre de l'Espagne*, p. 86.

Vaccination. — Canto I. st. 1.

It is odd that in Hindostan, where it might have been supposed superstition would have facilitated the introduction of this practice, a pious fraud was found necessary for removing the prejudice against it.

Mooperal Streenivaschary, a Brahmin, thus writes to Dr. Anderson, at Madras, on vaccine inoculation: —

"It might be useful to remove a prejudice in the minds of the people, arising from the term *cow-pock* being taken literally in our Tamul tongue; whereas there can be no doubt that it has been a drop of nectar from the exuberant udders of the cows in England, and no way similar to the humor discharged from the tongue and feet of diseased cattle in this country." — *Forbes's Oriental Memoirs*, vol. iii. p. 423.

For tyrannous fear dissolved all natural bonds of man.
Canto I. st. 3.

Mackenzie gives a dreadful picture of the effect of small-pox among the North-American Indians: —

"The small-pox spread its destructive and desolating power, as the fire consumes the dry grass of the field. The fatal infection spread around with a baneful rapidity, which no flight could escape, and with a fatal effect that nothing could resist. It destroyed with its pestilential breath whole families and tribes; and the horrid scene presented, to those who had the melancholy and afflicting opportunity of beholding it, a combination of the dead, the dying, and such as, to avoid the horrid fate of their friends around them, prepared to disappoint the plague of its prey, by terminating their own existence.

"The habits and lives of these devoted people, which provided not to-day for the wants of to-morrow, must have heightened the pains of such an affliction, by leaving them not only without remedy, but even without alleviation. Nought was left them but to submit in agony and despair.

"To aggravate the picture, if aggravation were possible, may be added the putrid carcasses which the wolves, with a furious voracity, dragged forth from the huts, or which were mangled within them by the dogs, whose hunger was satisfied with the disfigured remains of their masters. Nor was it uncommon for the father of a family, whom the infection had not reached, to call them around him to represent the cruel sufferings and horrid fate of their relations, from the influence of some evil spirit, who was preparing to extirpate their race; and to incite them to baffle death, with all its horrors, by their own poniards. At the same time, if their hearts failed them in this necessary act, he was himself ready to perform the deed of mercy with his own hand, as the last act of his affection, and instantly to follow them to the common place of rest and refuge from human evil."

And from the silent door the jaguar turns away.
Canto I. st. 11.

I may be forgiven for not having strictly adhered to natural history in this instance. The liberty which I have taken is mentioned, that it may not be supposed to have arisen from ignorance of this animal's habits.

The jaguar will not attack a living horse if a dead one be near; and, when it kills its prey, it drags it to its den, but is said not to eat the body till it becomes putrid. They are caught in large traps of the cage kind, baited with stinking meat, and then speared or shot through the bars. The Chalcaquines had a braver way of killing them: they provoked the animal, fronted it, received its attack upon a thick truncheon, which they held by the two ends, threw it down while its teeth were fixed in the wood, and ripped the creature up before it could recover. — *Techo*, p. 29. A great profit is made by their skins. The jaguar which has once tasted human flesh becomes a most formidable animal: such a beast is called a *tigre cevado*, — a fleshed tiger. There was one which infested the road between Santa Fé and Santiago, and had killed ten men; after which, a party of soldiers were sent to destroy it. The same thing is said of the lion and other beasts of prey, probably with truth; not, as is vulgarly supposed, because they have a particular appetite for this kind of food, but because, having once fed upon man, they from that time regard him, like any animal of inferior strength, as their natural prey. "It is a constant observation in Numidia," says Bruce, "that the lion avoids and flies from the face of men till by some accident they have been brought to engage, and the beast has prevailed against him: then that feeling of superiority, imprinted by the Creator in the heart of all animals, for man's preservation, seems to forsake him. The lion, having once tasted human blood, relinquishes the pursuit after the flock. He repairs to some highway or frequented path, and has been known, in the kingdom of Tunis, to interrupt the road to a market for several weeks; and in this he persists till hunters or soldiers are sent out to destroy him." Dobrizhoffer saw the skin of a jaguar which was as long as the standard hide. He says also that he saw one attack two horses which were coupled with a thong, kill one, and drag the other away after it.

A most unpleasant habit of this beast is, that, in cold or wet weather, he chooses to lodge within doors, and will steal into the house. A girl at Corrientes, who slept with her mother, saw one lying under the bed when she rose in the morning. She had presence of mind to bid her mother lie still, went for help, and soon rid the house of its perilous visitor. Cat-like, the jaguar is a good climber; but Dobrizhoffer tells us how a traveller who takes to a tree for shelter may profit by the position. "In promptu consilium; urina pro armis est: hac si tigridis ad arboris pedem minitantis oculos consperseris, salve res est. Quâ datâ portâ fuget illico." — i. 280. He who first did this must have been a good marksman as well as a cool fellow; and it was well for him that he reserved his fire till the jaguar was within shot.

Dobrizhoffer seems to credit an opinion (which is held in India of the tiger also) that the jaguar's claws are in a certain degree venomous: the scar which they leave is said to be always liable to a very painful and burning sense of heat. But that author, in his usual amusing manner, repeats many credulous notions concerning the animal, — as that its burnt claws are a remedy for the toothache; and that it has a mode of decoying fish, by standing neck-deep in the water, and spitting out a white foam, which allures them within reach. Techo (30) says the same thing of a large snake.

An opinion, that wounds inflicted by the stroke of animals of this kind are envenomed, is found in the East also. Capt. Williamson says, " However trivial the scratches made by the claws of tigers may appear, yet, whether it be owing to any noxious quality in the claw itself, to the manner in which the tiger strikes, or any other matter, I have no hesitation in saying, that at least a majority of such as have been under my notice died; and I have generally remarked, that those whose cases appeared the least alarming were most suddenly carried off. I have ever thought the perturbation arising from the nature of the attack to have a considerable share in the fatality alluded to, especially as I never knew any one wounded by a tiger to die without suffering for some days under that most dreadful symptom, — a locked jaw. Such as have been wounded to appearance severely, but accompanied with a moderate hemorrhage, I have commonly found to recover, excepting in the rainy season: at that period, I should expect serious consequences from either a bite or a scratch." — *Oriental Sports*, vol. i. p. 52.

Wild beasts were so numerous and fierce in one part of Mexico, among the Otomites, that Fr. Juan de Grijalva says in his time, in one year, more than two hundred and fifty Indians were devoured by them. " There then prevailed an opinion," he proceeds, " and still it prevails among many, that those tigers and lions were certain Indian sorcerers, whom they call Nahuales, who by diabolical art transform themselves into beasts, and tear the Indians in pieces, either to revenge themselves for some offences which they have received, or to do them evil; which is the proper condition of the Devil, and an effect of his fierceness. Some traces of these diabolical acts have been seen in our time; for, in the year 1579, the deaths of this kind being many, and the suspicion vehement, some Indians were put to the question; and they confessed the crime, and were executed for it. With all this experience and proof, there are many persons who doubt these transformations, and say that the land, being mountainous, produces wild beasts; and the beasts, being once fleshed, commit these great ravages. And it was through the weak understandings of the Indians that they were persuaded to believe their conjurers could thus metamorphose themselves; and, if these poor wretches confessed themselves guilty of such a crime, it was owing to their weakness under the torture; and so they suffered for an offence which they had never committed."

Father Grijalva, however, holds with his Father S. Augustine, who has said concerning such things, "Hæc ad nos non quibuscunque qualibus credere putaremus indignum, sed eis referentibus pervenerunt, quos nobis non existimaremus fuisse mentitos." "In the days of my Father S. Augustine," he says, "wonderful things were related of certain innkeepers in Italy, who transformed passengers into beasts of burden, to bring to their inns straw, barley, and whatever was wanted from the towns, and then metamorphosed them into their own persons, that they might purchase, as customers, the very commodities they had carried. And, in our times, the witches of Logrono make so many of these transformations, that now no one can doubt them. This matter of the Nahuales, or sorcerers of Tututepec, has been confessed by so many, that that alone suffices to make it credible. The best proof which can be had is, that they were condemned to death by course of justice; and it is temerity to condemn the judges, for it is to be believed that they made all due inquiry. Our brethren who have been ministers there, and are also judges of the interior court (that is, of the conscience), have all held these transformations to be certain; so that there ought to be no doubt concerning it. On the contrary, it is useful to understand it, that if at any time, in heathen lands, the Devil should work any of these metamorphoses, the Indians may see we are not surprised at them, and do not hold them as miraculous, but can explain to them the reason and cause of these effects, which astonish and terrify them so greatly."

He proceeds to show that the Devil can only exercise this

power as far as he is permitted by God, in punishment for sin, and that the metamorphosis is not real, but only apparent; the sorcerer not being actually transformed into a lion, but seeming as if he were so both to himself and others. In what manner he can tear a man really to pieces with imaginary claws, and devour him in earnest with an imaginary mouth, the good friar has not condescended to explain. — *Historia de la Orden de S. Augustin en la Provincia de N. España*, pp. 34, 35.

Preserved by horrid art,
In ghastly image of humanity! — Canto I. st. 13.

The more ghastly in proportion as more of the appearance of life is preserved in the revolting practice. Such, however, it was not to the feelings of the Egyptians, who had as much pride in a collection of their ancestors as one of the strongest family feeling could have in a collection of family pictures. "The body," Diodorus says, "is delivered to the kindred with every member so whole and entire, that no part of the body seems to be altered, even to the very hairs of the eyelids and the eyebrows, so that the beauty and shape of the face seems just as before. By which means, many of the Egyptians, laying up the bodies of their ancestors in stately monuments, perfectly see the true visage and countenance of those who were buried many ages before they themselves were born; so that, in regarding the proportion of every one of these bodies and the lineaments of their faces, they take exceeding great delight, even as if they were still living among them." — Book i.

They believe, says Herodotus ("Euterpe," § 123), that, on the dissolution of the body, the soul immediately enters into some other animal; and that, after using as vehicles every species of terrestrial, aquatic, and winged creatures, it finally enters a second time into a human body. They affirm that it undergoes all these changes in the space of three thousand years. This opinion some among the Greeks have at different periods of time adopted as their own; but I shall not, though I could, specify their names.

How little did the Egyptians apprehend that the bodies which they preserved with such care, to be ready again for use when the cycle should be fulfilled, would one day be regarded as an article of trade, broken up, exported piecemeal, and administered in grains and scruples, as a costly medicine, to rich patients! A preference was even given to virgin mummy.

The bodies of the Incas, from the founder of the empire, were preserved in the Temple of the Sun. They were seated each on his litter, and in such excellent preservation that they seemed to be alive, according to the testimony of P. Acosta and Garcilaso, who saw them, and touched them. It is not known in what manner they were prepared so as to resist the injuries of time. Gomara (c. 195) says they were embalmed by the juice of certain fragrant trees, which was poured down their throats, and by unguents of gum. Acosta says that a certain bitumen was used, and that plates of gold were placed instead of eyes, so well fitted that the want of the real eye was not perceived. Garcilaso thought the chief preparation consisted in freezing them with snow. They were buried in one of the courts of the Hospital of St. Andres. — *Merc. Peruano*, No. 221.

Hideous exhibitions of this kind are sometimes made in monasteries, where they are in perfect accord with monastic superstition. I remember seeing two human bodies, dry and shrivelled, suspended in the *Casas dos Ossos*, at Evora, a chapel, the walls of which are lined with skulls and bones.

"Among the remarkable objects in the vicinity of Palermo pointed out to strangers, they fail not to singularize a convent of Capuchins at a small distance from town, the beautiful gardens of which serve as a public walk. You are shown, under the fabric, a vault divided into four great galleries, into which the light is admitted by windows cut out at the top of each extremity. In this vault are preserved, not in flesh, but in skin and bone, all the Capuchins who have died in the convent since its foundation, as well as the bodies of several persons from the city. There are here private tombs belonging to opulent families, who, even after annihilation, disdain to be confounded with the vulgar part of mankind. It is said, that, in order to secure the preservation of these bodies, they are prepared by being gradually dried before a slow fire, so as to consume the flesh without greatly injuring the skin. When perfectly dry, they are invested with the Capuchin habit, and placed upright on tablets disposed step above step along the sides of the vault: the head, the arms, and the feet are left naked. A preservation like this is horrid; the skin discolored, dry, and as if it had been tanned, nay, torn in some places, glued close to the bones. It is easy to imagine from the different grimaces of this numerous assemblage of fleshless figures, rendered still more frightful by a long beard on the chin, what a hideous spectacle this must exhibit; and whoever has seen a Capuchin alive may form an idea of this singular repository of dead friars." — *Sonnini.*

It is not surprising that such practices arise from superstition; but it is strange, indeed, that they should afford any gratification to pride. That excellent man, Fletcher of Madeley, has a striking remark upon this subject. "The murderer," says he, "is dissected, in the surgeon's hall, gratis; and the rich sinner is embowelled in his own apartment at great expense. The robber, exposed to open air, wastes away in hoops of iron; and the gentleman, confined to a damp vault, moulders away in sheets of lead; and, while the fowls of the air greedily prey upon the one, the vermin of the earth eagerly devour the other."

How different is the feeling of the Hindoos upon this subject from that of the Egyptians! "A mansion with bones for its rafters and beams; with nerves and tendons for cords; with muscles and blood for mortar; with skin for its outward covering; filled with no sweet perfume, but loaded with fæces and urine; a mansion infested by age and by sorrow; the seat of malady, harassed with pains, haunted with the quality of darkness, and incapable of standing long. Such a mansion of the vital soul lets its occupier always cheerfully quit." — *Inst. of Menu.*

When the laden bee
Buzzed by him in its flight, he could pursue
Its path with certain ken. — Canto I. st. 20.

It is difficult to account for the superior quickness of sight which savages appear to possess. The Brazilian tribes used to eradicate the eyelashes and eyebrows, as impeding it. "Some Indians," P. Andres Perez de Ribas says, "were so quick-sighted, that they could ward off the coming arrow with their own bow." — L. ii. c. 3, p. 41.

Covering with soft gums the obedient limb
And body, then with feathers overlay,
In regular hues disposed. — Canto I. st. 25.

Inconvenient as this may seem, it was the full dress of the Tupi and Guarani tribes. A fashion less gorgeous and elaborate, but more refined, is described by one of the best old travellers to the East, — François Pyrard.

"The inhabitants of the Maldives use on feast-days this kind of gallantry. They bruise sanders (sandal-wood) and camphire on very slicke and smooth stones (which they bring from the firm land), and sometimes other sorts of odoriferous woods. After, they compound it with water distilled of flowers, and overspread their bodies with this paste, from the girdle upwards; adding many forms with their fingers, such as they imagine. It is somewhat like cut and pinked doublets, and of an excellent savor. They dress their wives or lemans in this sort, and make upon their backs works and shadows as they please." Skin-prints Purchas calls this. — *Pyrard de Laval. Purchas*, p. 1655.

The abominable practice of tarring and feathering was but too well known during the American war. It even found its way to England. I remember, when a child, to have seen a man in this condition in the streets of Bristol.

The costume of the savages, who figured so frequently in the pageants of the sixteenth century, seems to have been designed to imitate the Brazilian tribes, best known to the French and English at that time. Indeed, this is stated by Vincent Carloix, when, in describing an entertainment given to Marechal de Vieilleville by the captains of the galleys at Marseilles, he says, "Ayant lié six galères ensemble de front, et faict dresser les tables dessus, et tapissées en façon de grandes salles; ayant accoustrés les forceats en Bressiliens pour servir, ils firent une infinité de gambades et de tourbions à la façon des sauvages, que personne n'avoit encore veues; dont tout le monde, avec une extresme allaigresse, s'esbahissoit merveilleusement." — *Mémoires*, l. x. ch. 18.

Drinking-feasts. — Canto I. st. 26.

"The point of honor in drinking is not the same among the savages of Guiana as among the English potators: they account him that is drunk first the bravest fellow." — *Harcourt's Voyage.*

A custom strange, and yet far spread
Through many a savage tribe, howe'er it grew,
And once in the Old World known as widely as the New.
Canto I. st. 28.

"Je la trouve chez les Ibériens, ou les premiers peuples d'Espagne; je la trouve chez les anciens habitans de l'Isle de Corse. Elle étoit chez les Tibareniens en Asie; elle est aujourd'hui dans quelques unes de nos provinces voisines d'Espagne, où cela s'appelle faire couvade; elle est encore vers le Japon, et dans l'Amérique chez les Caraibes et les Galibis." — *Lafitau: Mœurs des Sauvages*, t. i. p. 50.

Strabo says, this strange custom existed in Cantabria (l. iii. p. 174, ed. 1571), so that its Gascon extraction has been direct. Diodorus Siculus is the authority for its existence in Corsica (book iii. ch. 1, English translation, 1814, vol. i. p. 305). Apollonius Rhodius describes it among the Tibareni (l. ii. 1012): *ὡς ἱστορεῖ Νυμφόδωρος ἐν τισιν νόμοις*, says the scholiast.

"Voicy la brutalité de nos sauvages dans leurs réjouissances pour l'accroissement de leur famille. C'est qu'au même tems que la femme est délivrée, le mary se met au lit, pour s'y plaindre et y faire l'accouchée; coutume, que bien que sauvage et ridicule, se trouve néantmoins, à ce que l'on dit, parmy les paysans d'une certaine province de France; et ils appellent cela *faire la couvade.* Mais ce qui est de fâcheuse pour le pauvre Caraibe que s'est mis au lit au lieu de l'accouchée, c'est qu'on luy fait faire diète dix ou douze jours de suite, ne luy donnant rien par jour qu'un morceau de cassave, et un peu d'eau dans laquelle on a aussi fait boullir un peu de ce pain de racine. Après il mange un peu plus; mais il n'entame la cassave que luy est présentée que par le milieu durant quelques quarante jours, en laissant les bords entiers qu'il pend à sa case, pour servir à un festin qu'il fait ordinairement en suite à tous ses amis. Et même il s'abstient après cela, quelquefois dix mois ou un an entier de plusieurs viandes, comme de lamantin, de tortuë, de pourceau, de poules, de poisson, et de choses délicates, craignant par une pitoyable folie que cela ne nuise à l'enfant. Mais ils ne font ce grand jusne qu'à la naissance de leur premier enfant." — *Rochefort: Hist. Morale des Isles Antilles*, c. xxiii. p. 495.

Marco Polo (l. ii. c. 41), the other authority to which Lafitau refers, speaks of the custom as existing in the great khan's province of Cardandan. "Hanno un' usanza che subito ch' una donna ha partorito, si leva del letto, e lavato il fanciullo e ravolto ne' panni, il marito si mette a giacere in letto in sua vece, e tiene il figliuolo appresso di se, havendo la cura di quello per quaranta giorni, che non si parte mai. Et gli amici e parenti vanno a visitarlo per rallegrarlo e consolarlo; e le donne che sono da parto fanno quel che bisogna per casa, portando da mangiare e bere al marito, ch' e nel letto, e dando il latte al fanciullo, che gli è appresso." — *Ramusio*, t. ii. p. 36, ed. 1583.

Yet this custom, preposterous as it is, is not more strange than an opinion which was once so prevalent in this country, that Primerose made it the subject of a chapter in his work, "De Vulgi Erroribus in Medicinâ," and thought it necessary to prove, by physical reasons, "maritum loco uxoris gravidæ non ægrotare;" for such is the title of one of his chapters. He says, "Inter errores quamplurimos maximè ridendus hic esse videtur, quod vir credatur ægrotare, iisque affici symptomatis, quibus ipsa mulier prægnans solet, illudque experientiâ confirmatum plurimi esse volunt. Habebam ægrum febre laborentem cum urinâ valde accensâ et turbidâ, qui ægrotationis suæ nullam causam agnoscebat quam uxoris suæ graviditatem. Nullibi terrarum quam in Angliâ id observatum memini me audivisse, aut legisse unquam. — Nec si quis maritus cum uxor gravida est, ægrotat ab uxore infectus fuit, sed potest ex peculiari proprii corporis vitio id pati. Sicut dum hæc scribo, pluit; non est tamen pluvia aut causa scriptionis, aut scriptura pluviæ. Res nova non est, viros et mulieres etiam simul ægrotare. At mirum est hactenusque ignotum, graviditatem affectum esse contagiosum, et non alias mulieres sed viros, quos natura immunes ab hoc labore fecit, solos infici. Præterea observatum est non omnibus mulieribus ejusmodi symptomata, aut saltem non omnia singulis contingere; et tamen accidit sæpe ut cum mulier bene valet, ægrotet maritus, etiam absens per aliquot milliaria. Sed quoniam ex solâ relatione absurditas hujus erroris patet, plura non addam. Jupiter Bacchum in femore, Palladem in cerebro gestavit. Sed hoc illi esto proprium." — Lib. ii. c. 13.

This notion, however, is probably not yet extinct; for I know that it existed in full force some thirty years ago, and that not in the lowest rank of life.

Till hardened mothers in the grave could lay
Their living babes with no compunctious tear.

Canto I. st. 38.

This dreadful practice is carried to such an extent in the heart of South America, that whole tribes have become extinct in consequence of it, and of another practice hardly less nefarious.

Those bloody African savages, the Giagas, reared no children whatsoever; "for as soon," says Battell, "as the woman is delivered of her child, it is presently buried quick; so that there is not one child brought up in all this generation. But, when they take any town, they keep the boys and girls of thirteen or fourteen years of age as their own children; but the men and women they kill and eat. These little boys they train up in the wars, and hang a collar about their necks for a disgrace, which is never taken off till he proveth himself a man, and brings his enemy's head to the general; and then it is taken off, and he is a free man, and is called '*gonso*,' or 'soldier.' This maketh them all desperate and forward to be free, and counted men; and so they do increase." "A generation without generation," says Purchas, p. 977.

Among the causes for which the Knisteneaux women procure abortion, Mackenzie (p. 98) assigns that of hatred for the father. No other traveller has ever suspected the existence of this motive. They sometimes kill their female children to save them from the miseries which they themselves have suffered.

"The practice among the Panches of Bogota was, that, if the first-born proved a girl, it was destroyed, and every girl in succession till the mother bore a boy; after which, girls were allowed to live: but, if the first-born were a boy, all the children then were reared." — *Piedrahita*, p. 11.

Perhaps the most flagitious motive for which this crime has ever become a practice is that which the Guana women assign for it: they destroy the greater number of their female infants, in order to keep up the value of the sex. — *Azara*, t. ii. 85–100. See *Hist. of Brazil*, vol. ii. 379. A knowledge of the evils which polygamy brings upon some of their neighbors may have led to this mode of preventing it.

Father Gumilla one day bitterly reproved a Betoya woman (whom he describes as having more capacity than any other of the Indians in those parts) for killing her new-born daughter. She listened to him without lifting her eyes from the ground; and when he had done, and thought that she was convinced of her guilt, and heartily repented of it, she said, "Father, if you will not be angry, I will tell you what is in my heart." He promised that he would not, and bade her speak freely. "This she said to me," he says, "as follows, literally translated from the Betoya tongue: 'Would to God, Father, would to God, my mother when she brought me forth had loved me so well and pitied me so much as to have saved me from all those troubles which I have endured till this day, and am to endure till death! If my mother had buried me as soon as I was born, I should have died, but should not have felt death, and should have been spared from that death which must come, and should have escaped so many things bitterer than death: who knows how many more such I must endure before I die? Consider well, Father, the hardships that a poor Indian woman endures among these Indians. They go with us to the plantations; but they have a bow and arrow in their hands, — nothing more. We go with a basketful of things on the back, one child at the breast, another upon the basket. Their business is to shoot a bird or a fish; ours is to dig and work in the field. At evening, they go home without any burden: we, besides our children, have to carry roots for their food, and maize to make their drink. They, when they reach the house, go to converse with their friends: we have to seek wood, fetch water, and prepare their supper. Having supped, they go to sleep; but we, almost all the night, are pounding maize to make their *chica:* And what is the end of this our watching and labor? They drink the *chica;* they get drunk, and, being out of their senses, beat us with sticks, take us by the hair, drag us about, and trample on us. Would to God, Father, that my mother had buried me when she brought me forth! You know that I complain with cause; for all that I have said you witness every day. But our greatest pain you do not know, because you never can suffer it. You do not know, Father, the death it is for the poor Indian woman, when having served her husband as a slave, sweating in the field, and in the house without sleep, at the end of twenty years she sees him take a girl for another wife. Her he loves; and, though she ill uses our children, we cannot interfere; for he neither loves us nor cares for us now. A girl is to command over us, and treat us as her servants; and, if we speak, they silence us with sticks. Can any Indian woman do better for the daughter which she brings forth than to save it from all these troubles, and deliver it from this slavery, worse than death? I say again, Father, would to God my mother had made me feel her kindness by burying me as soon as I was born! Then would not this heart have had now so much to feel, nor these eyes so much to weep for.'

"Here," says Gumilla, "tears put an end to her speech; and the worst is, that all which she said, and all she would have said if grief had allowed her to proceed, is true." — *Orinoco Ilustrado*, t. ii. p. 65, ed. 1791.

From the dove,
They named the child Yeruti. — Canto I. st. 42.

This is the Guarani name for the species described by Azara, t. iv. p. 130, No. cccxx.

What Power had placed them here. — Canto II. st. 27.

"Some of the Orinoco tribes believe that their first forefathers grew upon trees." — *Gumilla*, t. i. c. 6.

"The Othomacas, one of the rudest of the Orinoco tribes, suppose themselves descended from a pile of stones upon the top of a rock called Barraguan, and that they all return to stone as they came from it; so that this mass of rock is composed of their forefathers. Therefore, though they bury their dead, within the year they take off their heads, and carry them to the holes in the rock." — *Gumilla*, t. i. c. 6.

"These are the odd people who always for a first marriage give a girl to an old man, and a youth to an old woman. Polygamy is not in use among them; and they say, that, if the young people came together, there could be no good household management." — *Gumilla*, t. i. c. 12.

P. Labbé (*Lett. Edif.* t. viii. p. 180, edit. 1781) speaks of a tribe on the north bank of the Plata who put their women to death when they were thirty years old, thinking they had then lived long enough. I have not seen this custom mentioned by any other writer, nor do I believe that it can possibly have existed.

And Father was his name. — Canto II. st. 28.

"Tupa. It is the Tupi and Guarani name for Father, for Thunder, and for the Supreme Being.

"The Patagones call the Supreme Being *Soychu*, — a word which is said to express that which cannot be seen, which is worthy of all veneration, and which is out of the world. They may thus explain the word; but it cannot contain this meaning: it is a definition of what they mean, and apparently not such as a savage would give. The dead they call *Soychuhet;* they who are with God, and out of the world.

"The Puelches, Picunches, and Moluches have no name for God. Their prayers are made to the sun, whom they regard as the giver of all good. A Jesuit once admonished them to worship that God who created all things, and this orb among the rest; but they replied, they had never known any thing greater or better than the sun." — *Dobrizhoffer*, t. ii. p. 100.

The most remarkable mode of superstition I remember to have met with is one which is mentioned by the Bishop of Santa Marta, in his "History of the Nuevo Reyno de Granada." He tells us that "the Pijaos of the Nuevo Reyno worshipped nothing visible or invisible, except the spirits of those whom they killed for the purpose of deifying them. For they thought, that, if an innocent person were put to death, he became a god, and in that capacity would be grateful to those who were the authors of his apotheosis. For this reason, they used to catch strangers and kill them; not thinking one of their own horde, or of their enemies, could be esteemed innocent, and therefore fitting. A woman or a child would do. But after a few months they held it necessary to make a new god; the old one either having lost his power, or changed his place, or perhaps by that time discharged himself of his debt of gratitude." — *Piedrahita*, p. 12.

And once there was a way to that good land;
For in mid-earth a wondrous Tree there grew.
Canto II. st. 33.

"Los Mocobis fingian un Arbol, que en su idioma llamaban Nalliagdigua, de altura tan desmedida que llegaba desde la tierra al cielo. Por el de rama en rama ganando siempre maior elevacion subian las almas á pezcar de un rio y lagunas muy grandes, que abundaban de pescado regaladisimo. Pero un dia que el alma de una Vieja no pudo pescar cosa alguna, y los pescadores la negaron el socorro de una limosna para su mantenimiento, se irritó tanto contra la nacion Mocobi que, transfiguranda en Capiguara tomó el exercicio de roer el Arbol por donde subian al cielo, y no desistió hasta derribarlo en tierra con increible sentimiento y dano irreparable de toda la nacion."

This legend is contained in a manuscript history of Paraguay, the Rio de la Plata, and Tucuman. For the use of the first volume (a transcript of which is in my possession), I am beholden, as for other civilities of the same kind, to Mr. Thomas Kinder. This portion of the work contains a good account of the native tribes; the second volume contains the historical part: but, when Mr. Kinder purchased the one at Buenos Ayres the other was on its way to the United States, having been borrowed from the owner by an American, and not returned. Fortunately the subjects of the two volumes are so distinct, that each may be considered as a complete work; and I have referred, in the history of Brazil, to that which I possess, by the title of *Noticias del Paraguay*, &c.

The Land of Souls. — Canto II. st. 39.

Many of the Indian speculations respecting the condition of souls in a future state are given in my "History of Brazil." A description of a Keltic Island of the Blessed, as dressed up by Ossian Macpherson, may be found in the notes to "Madoc." A Tonga one is thus described in the very curious and valuable work of Mr. Mariner: —

"The Tonga people universally and positively believe in the existence of a large island lying at a considerable distance to the north-west of their own islands, which they consider to be the place of residence of their gods, and of the souls of their nobles and mataboohes. This island is supposed to be much larger than all their own islands put together; to be well stocked with all kinds of useful and ornamental plants, always in a state of high perfection, and always bearing the richest fruits and the most beautiful flowers, according to their respective natures; that, when these fruits or flowers are plucked, others immediately occupy their place; and that the whole atmosphere is filled with the most delightful fragrance that the imagination can conceive, proceeding from these immortal plants. The island is also well stocked with the most beautiful birds of all imaginable kinds, as well as with abundance of hogs, all of which are immortal, unless they are killed to provide food for the Hotooas, or gods: but, the moment a hog or bird is killed, another living hog or bird immediately comes into existence to supply its place, the same as with the fruits and flowers; and this, as far as they know or suppose, is the only mode of propagation of plants and animals. The Island of Bolotoo is supposed to be so far off as to render it dangerous for their canoes to attempt going there; and it is supposed, moreover, that even if they were to succeed in reaching so far, unless it happened to be the particular will of the gods, they would be sure to miss it. They give, however, an account of a Tonga canoe, which, in her return from the Feejee Islands a long time ago, was driven by stress of weather to Bolotoo. Ignorant of the place where they were, and being much in want of provisions, and seeing the country abound in all sorts of fruit, the crew landed, and proceeded to pluck some bread-fruit; but, to their unspeakable astonishment, they could no more lay hold of it than if it were a shadow. They walked through the trunks of the trees, and passed through the substance of the houses (which were built like those of Tonga), without feeling any resistance. They at length saw some of the Hotooas, who passed through the substance of their bodies as if there was nothing there. The Hotooas recommended them to go away immediately, as they had no proper food for them, and promised them a fair wind and a speedy passage. They accordingly put directly to sea; and in two days, sailing with the utmost velocity, they arrived at Hamoa (the Navigators' Island), at which place they wanted to touch before they got to Tonga. Having remained at Hamoa two or three days, they sailed for Tonga, where they arrived with great speed: but, in the course of a few days, they all died, not as a punishment for having been at Bolotoo, but as a natural consequence; the air of Bolotoo, as it were, infecting mortal bodies with speedy death."

"In Yucatan, their notion of the happy after death was, that they rested in a delightful land, under the shade of a great tree, where there was plenty of food and drink." — *Herrera*, iv. 10, n.

"The Austral tribes believe that the dead live in some region under the earth, where they have their tents, and hunt the souls of ostriches." — *Dobrizh.*, ii. 295.

The Persians have a great reverence for large, old trees, thinking that the souls of the happy delight to dwell in them; and, for this reason, they call them *Pir*, which signifies an old man; by which name they also designate the supposed inhabitant. Pietro Della Valle describes a prodigious tree of this character, in the hollow of which tapers were always kept burning to the honor of the *Pir*. He pitched his tent under its boughs twice, — once with his wife when on his way to embark for Europe, and again when returning with her corpse. The passage wherein he speaks of this last night's lodging is very affecting. We soon forgive this excellent traveller for his coxcombry, take an interest in his domestic affairs, and part with him at last as with an old friend.

Who thought
From Death, as from some living foe, to fly. — Canto II. st. 44.

An opinion of this kind has extended to people in a much higher grade of society than the American Indians.

"After this, DEATH appeared in Dwaraka in a human shape, the color of his skin being black and yellow, his head close shorn, and all his limbs distorted. He placed himself at men's doors, so that all those who saw him shuddered with apprehension, and became even as dead men from mere affright. Every person to whose door he came shot an arrow at him; and, the moment the arrow quitted the bowstring, they saw the spectre no more, nor knew which way he was gone." — *Life of Creeshna.*

This is a poetical invention; but such an invention has formed a popular belief in Greece, if M. Pouqueville may be trusted.

"The *Evil Eye*, the *Cacodæmon*, has been seen wandering over the roofs of the houses. Who can dare to doubt this? It was in the form of a withered old woman, covered with funeral rags: she was heard to call by their names those who are to be cut off from the number of the living. Nocturnal concerts, voices murmuring amid the silence of the darkest nights, have been heard in the air; phantoms have been seen wandering about in solitary places, in the streets, in the markets; the dogs have howled with the most dismal and melancholy tone, and their cries have been repeated by the echoes along the desert streets. It is when such things happen, as I was told very seriously by an inhabitant of Nauplia di Romania, that great care must be taken not to answer if you should be called during the night. If you hear symphonies, bury yourself in the bed-clothes, and do not listen to them: it is the *Old Woman*, it is the Plague itself, that knocks at your door." — *Pouqueville*, 189.

"The Patagones, and other Austral tribes, attribute all diseases to an evil spirit. Their conjurers therefore beat drums by the patient, which have hideous figures painted upon them, thinking thus to frighten away the cause. If he dies, his relations endeavor to take vengeance upon those who pretended to cure him; but, if one of the chiefs dies, all the conjurers are slain, unless they can save themselves by flight." — *Dobrizhoffer*, t. ii. 286.

They dragged the dying out. — Canto II. st. 45.

The Austral tribes sometimes bury the dying, thinking it an act of mercy thus to shorten their sufferings. — *Dobrizh.*, t. ii. 286. But, in general, this practice, which extends widely among savages, arises from the selfish feeling assigned in the text. Superstition, without this selfishness, produces a practice of the same kind, though not absolutely as brutal, in the East. "The *moorda* or *chultries* are small huts, in which a Hindoo, when given over by his physicians, is deposited, and left alone to expire, and be carried off by the sacred flood." — *Cruso, in Forbes*, iv. 99.

"When there is no hope of recovery, the patient is generally removed from the bed, and laid on a platform of fresh earth, either out of doors, or prepared purposely in some adjoining room or veranda, that he may there breathe his last. In a physical sense, this removal at so critical a period must be often attended with fatal consequences, though perhaps not quite so decisive as that of exposing an aged parent or a dying friend on the banks of the Ganges. I now only mention the circumstances as forming part of the Hindoo religious system. After having expired upon the earth, the body is carried to the water-side, and washed with many ceremonies. It is then laid upon the funeral pile, that the fire may have a share of the victim: the ashes are finally scattered in the air, and fall upon the water.

"During the funeral ceremony, which is solemn and affecting, the Brahmins address the respective elements in words to the following purport, although there may be a different mode of performing these religious rites in other parts of Hindostan: —

"O Earth! to thee we commend our brother: of thee he was formed; by thee he was sustained; and unto thee he now returns.

"O Fire! thou hadst a claim in our brother: during his life, he subsisted by thy influence in nature. To thee we commit his body. Thou emblem of purity, may his spirit be purified on entering a new state of existence!

"O Air! while the breath of life continued, our brother respired by thee. His last breath is now departed. To thee we yield him.

"O Water! thou didst contribute to the life of our brother: thou wert one of his sustaining elements. His remains are now dispersed. Receive thy share of him, who has now taken an everlasting flight!" — *Forbes's Oriental Memoirs*, iii. 12.

Her feet upon the crescent Moon were set. — Canto II. st. 51.

This is a common representation of the Virgin, from the Revelation.

> Virgem de Sol vestida, e dos seus raios
> Claros envolta toda, e das Estrellas
> Coroada, e debaixo os pés a Lua.
>
> *Francisco de Sa de Miranda.*

These lines are highly esteemed by the Portuguese critics.

Severe he was, and in his anger dread,
Yet alway at his Mother's will grew mild,
So well did he obey that Maiden undefiled.

Canto II. st. 51.

'How hath the conceit of Christ's humiliation here on earth, of his dependence on his *mother* during the time of his formation and birth, and of his subjection to *her* in his infancy, brought forth preposterous and more than heathenish transformations of his glory in the superstitious daughters of the idolatrous church! They cannot conceive Christ as King, unless they acknowledge her as Queen Dowager of heaven: her title of Lady is æquiparant to his title of Lord; her authority for some purposes held as great, her bowels of compunction (towards the weaker sex especially) more tender. And as the heathens frame gods suitable to their own desire, soliciting them most (though otherwise less potent) whom they conceive to be most favorable to their present suits; so hath the blessed Virgin, throughout the Romish church, obtained (what she never sought) the entire monopoly of women's prayers in their travails; as if her presence at others' distressful labors (for she herself, by their doctrine, brought forth her first-born and only son without pain) had wrought in her a truer feeling or ten derer touch than the High Priest of their souls can have of their infirmities, or as if she would use more faithful and effectual intercession with her Son than he can or will do with his Father! Some in our times, out of the weakness of their sex, matching with the impetuousness of their adulterous and disloyal zeal, have in this kind been so impotently outrageous as to intercept others' supplications directed to Christ, and *superscribe* them in this form unto his mother: '*Blessed Lady*, command thy son to hear this woman's prayers, and send her deliverance!' These and the like speeches have moved some good women, in other points tainted rather with superstition than preciseness, to dispense with the law of secrecy, seldom violated in their parliaments; and I know not whether I should attribute it to their courage or stupidity not to be more affrighted at such blasphemies than at some monstrous and prodigious birth. This and the like inbred inclinations unto superstition, in the rude and uninstructed people, are more artificially set forward by the fabulous Roman legendary and his limner, than the like were in the heathen by heathen poets and painters." — *Dr. Thomas Jackson's Works*, vol. i. 1007.

Tyranny of the Spaniards. — Canto III. st. 7, 8.

The consumption of the Indians in the Paraguay tea-trade, and the means taken by the Jesuits for cultivating the Caa-tree, are described by Dobrizhoffer.

The Encomenderos compelled the unhappy people, whom they found living where they liked, to settle in such places as were most convenient for the work in which they were now to be compulsorily employed. All their work was task-work, imposed with little moderation, and exacted without mercy. This tyranny extended to the women and children; and as all the Spaniards, the officers of justice as well as the Encomenderos, were implicated in it, the Indians had none to whom they could look for protection. Even the institutions of Christianity, by which the Spanish government hoped to better the temporal condition of its new subjects, were made the occasion of new grievances, and more intolerable oppression. For, as the Indians were legally free, — free, therefore, to marry where they pleased, and the wife was to follow the husband, — every means was taken to prevent a marriage between two Indians who belonged to different *Repartimientos;* and the interest of the master counteracted all the efforts of the priest. The Spanish women are said to have exceeded their husbands in cruelty on such occasions, and to have instigated them to the most violent and iniquitous measures, that they might not lose their female attendants. The consequence was, that profligacy of manners among the Indians was rather encouraged than restrained, as it is now in the English sugar-islands, where the planter is not a religious man." — *Lozano,* l. i. § 3, 6, 7.

And she, in many an emulous essáy,
At length into a descant of her own
Had blended all their notes, &c. — Canto III. st. 39, &c.

An extract from a journal written in Switzerland will be the best comment upon the description in these stanzas; which, indeed, were probably suggested by my recollections of the Staubach.

"While we were at the waterfall, some half-score peasants, chiefly women and girls, assembled just out of reach of the spray, and set up — surely the wildest chorus that ever was heard by human ears — a song, not of articulate sounds, but in which the voice was used as a mere instrument of music, more flexible than any which art could produce, — sweet, powerful, and thrilling beyond description."

It will be seen by the subjoined sonnet of Mr. Wordsworth's, who visited this spot three years after me, that he was not less impressed than I had been by this wild concert of voices: —

" *On approaching the Staub-bach, Lauterbrunnen.*

" Tracks let me follow far from human-kind
Which these illusive greetings may not reach;
Where only Nature tunes her voice to teach
Careless pursuits, and raptures unconfined.
No Mermaid warbles (to allay the wind
That drives some vessel towards a dangerous beach)
More thrilling melodies! no caverned Witch,
Chanting a love-spell, ever intertwined
Notes shrill and wild with art more musical!
Alas that from the lips of abject Want
And Idleness, in tatters mendicant,
They should proceed, — enjoyment to inthrall,
And with regret and useless pity haunt
This bold, this pure, this sky-born waterfall! "

" The vocal powers of these musical beggars," says Mr. Wordsworth, " may seem to be exaggerated; but this wild and savage air was utterly unlike any sounds I had ever heard. The notes reached me from a distance; and on what occasion they were sung, I could not guess; only they seemed to belong in some way or other to the waterfall, and reminded me of religious services chanted to streams and fountains in Pagan times."

Some dim preságe. — Canto III. st. 41.

Upon this subject an old Spanish romancer speaks thus: " Aunque hombre no sabe lo de adelante como ha de venir, el espiritu lo siente, y antes que venga se duele dello: y de aqui se levantaron los grandes sospiros que hombres dan á sobrevienta no pensando en ninguna cosa, como á muchos acaesce; que aquel que el sospiro echa de si, el espiritu es que siente el mal que ha de ser." — *Chronica del Rey D. Rodrigo*, p. ii. c. 171.

Across her shoulders was a hammock flung. — Canto III. st. 45.

Pinkerton, in his Geography (vol. ii. p. 535, n. 3d edit.), says that nets are sometimes worn among the Guaranis instead of clothes, and refers to this very story in proof of his assertion. I believe he had no other ground for it. He adds, that "perhaps they were worn only to keep off the flies;" as if those blood-suckers were to be kept off by open net-work!

We owe something, however, to the person who introduces us to a good and valuable book; and I am indebted originally to Mr. Pinkerton for my knowledge of Dobrizhoffer. He says of him, when referring to the *Historia de Abiponibus*, "The lively singularity of the old man's Latin is itself an amusement; and, though sometimes garrulous, he is redundant in authentic and curious information. His work, though bearing a restricted title, is the best account yet published of the whole viceroyalty of La Plata."

St. Joachin. — Canto IV. st. 17.

The legend of his visit to Limbo is given here in a translated extract from that very curious work, the "Life of the Virgin Mary, as related by herself to Sister Maria de Jesus, Abbess of the Franciscan Convent de la Inmaculada Concepcion at Agreda," and published with the sanction of all the ecclesiastical authorities in Spain.

After some conversation between the Almighty and the Virgin, at that time three years and a half old, the Franciscan confessor, who was the accomplice of the abbess in this blasphemous imposture, proceeds thus: —

"The Most High received, this morning, sacrifice from his tender spouse, Mary the most holy, and with a pleased countenance said to her, 'Thou art beautiful in thy thoughts, O Prince's daughter! my dove, and my beloved. I admit thy desires, which are agreeable to my eyes; and it is my will, in fulfilment of them, that thou shouldest understand the time draws nigh, when, by my divine appointment, thy father Joachin must pass from this mortal life to the life immortal and eternal. His death shall be short; and he will soon rest in peace, and be placed with the saints in Limbo, awaiting the redemption of the whole human race.' This information from the Lord neither disturbed nor troubled the regal breast of Mary, the Princess of Heaven; yet as the love of children to their parents is a debt due by nature, and that love in all its perfection existed in this most holy child, a natural grief at losing her most holy father Joachin, whom as a daughter she devoutly loved, could not fail to be resented. The tender and sweet child Mary felt a movement of grief compatible with the serenity of her magnanimous heart; and acting with greatness in every thing, following both grace and nature, she made a fervent prayer for her father Joachin: she besought the Lord, that, as the mighty and true God, he would look upon him in the hour of his happy death, and defend him from the Devil, especially in that hour, and preserve him, and appoint him in the number of his elect, as one who in his life had confessed and magnified his holy and adorable name. And, the more to oblige his Majesty, the most faithful daughter offered to endure for her father, the most holy Joachin, all that the Lord might ordain.

"His Majesty accepted this petition, and consoled the divine child, assuring her that he would be with her father as a merciful and compassionate remunerator of those who love and serve him, and that he would place him with the patriarchs, Abraham, Isaac, and Jacob; and he prepared her again to receive and suffer other troubles. Eight days before the death of the holy patriarch Joachin, Mary the most holy had other advices from the Lord, declaring the day and hour in which he was to die; as in fact it occurred, only six months after our Queen went to reside in the temple. When her Highness had received this information from the Lord, she besought the twelve angels (who, I have before said, were those whom St. John names in the Revelation) that they would be with her father Joachin in his sickness, and comfort him and console him in it; and thus they did. And, for the last hour of his transit, she sent all those of her guard, and besought the Lord that he would make them manifest to her father for his greater consolation. The Most High granted this, and in every thing fulfilled the desire of his elect, unique, and perfect one; and the great patriarch and happy Joachin saw the thousand holy angels who guarded his daughter Maria, at whose petition and desire the grace of the Almighty superabounded, and by his command the Angels said to Joachin these things: —

"'Man of God, the Most High and Mighty is thy eternal salvation; and he sends thee from his holy place the necessary and timely assistance for thy soul! Mary, thy daughter, sends us to be with thee at this hour, in which thou hast to pay to thy Creator the debt of natural death. She is thy most faithful and powerful intercessor with the Most High, in whose name and peace depart thou from this world with consolation and joy, that he hath made thee parent of so blessed a daughter. And although his incomprehensible Majesty, in his serene wisdom, hath not till now manifested to thee the sacrament and dignity in which he will constitute thy daughter, it is his pleasure that thou shouldest know it now, to the intent that thou mayest magnify him and praise him, and that at such news the jubilee of thy spirit may be joined with the grief and natural sadness of death. Mary, thy daughter and our Queen, is the one chosen by the arm of the Omnipotent, that the Divine Word may in her clothe himself with flesh, and with the human form. She is to be the happy Mother of the Messiah, blessed among women, superior to all creatures, and inferior only to God himself. Thy most happy daughter is to be the repairer of what the human race lost by the first fall, and the high mountain whereon the new law of grace is to be formed and established. Therefore, as thou leavest now in the world its restauratrix and daughter, by whom God prepares for it the fitting remedy, depart thou in joy; and the Lord will bless thee from Zion, and will give thee a place among the Saints, that thou mayest attain to the sight and possession of the happy Jerusalem.'

" While the holy Angels spake these words to Joachin, St. Anna, his wife, was present, standing by the pillow of his bed, and she heard, and, by divine permission, understood them. At the same time, the holy Patriarch Joachin lost his speech, and, entering upon the common way of all flesh, began to die, with a marvellous struggle between the light of such joyful tidings and the pain of death. During this conflict with his interior powers, many and fervent acts of divine love, of faith and adoration and praise and thanksgiving and humiliation, and other virtues, did he heroically perform; and, thus absorbed in the new knowledge of so divine a mystery, he came to the end of his natural life, dying the precious death of the Saints. His most holy spirit was carried by the Angels to the Limbo of the Holy Fathers and of the Just; and, for a new consolation and light in the long night wherein they dwelt, the Most High ordered that the soul of the holy Patriarch Joachin should be the new Paranymph and Ambassador of his Great Majesty for announcing to all that great congregation of the Just how the day of eternal light had now dawned, and the daybreak was born, — Mary, the most holy daughter of Joachin and of Anna, from whom should be born the Sun of Divinity, Christ, Restorer of the whole human race. The Holy Fathers and the Just in Limbo heard these tidings, and, in their jubilee, composed new hymns of thanksgiving to the Most High.

"This happy death of the Patriarch St. Joachin occurred (as I have before said) half a year after his daughter, Mary the most holy, entered the Temple; and, when she was at the tender age of three and a half, she was thus left in the world without a natural father. The age of the patriarch was sixty and nine years, distributed and divided thus: At the age of forty-six years, he took St. Anna to wife; twenty years after this marriage, Mary the most holy was born; and the three years and a half of her Highness's age make sixty-nine and a half, a few days more or less.

"The holy Patriarch and father of our Queen being dead, the holy Angels of her guard returned incontinently to her presence, and gave her notice of all that had occurred in her father's transit. Forthwith the most prudent child solicited with prayers for the consolation of her mother St. Anna, entreating that the Lord would, as a father, direct and govern her in the solitude wherein, by the loss of her husband Joachin, she was left. St. Anna herself sent also news of his death, which was first communicated to the Mistress of our divine Princess, that, in imparting it, she might console her. The Mistress did this; and the most wise child heard her with all composure and dissimulation, but with the patience and the modesty of a queen: but she was not ignorant of the event which her Mistress related to her as news." — *Mistica Ciudad de Dios*, par. 1, l. 2, c. 16, § 664–69. Madrid, 1744.

It was in the middle of the seventeenth century that the work from which this extract is translated was palmed upon the Spaniards as a new revelation. Gross and blasphemous as the imposture is, the work was still current when I procured my copy about twenty years ago; and it is not included in the Spanish Index Expurgatorius of 1790, the last (I believe) which was published, and which is now before me.

He could not tarry here. — Canto IV. st. 67.

A case precisely of the same kind is mentioned by Mr. Mariner: "A young chief at Tonga, a very handsome man, was inspired by the ghost of a woman in Bolotoo, who had fallen in love with him. On a sudden he felt himself low-spirited, and, shortly afterwards, fainted away. When he came to himself, he was very ill, and was taken accordingly to the house of a priest. As yet, he did not know who it was that inspired him; but the priest informed him that it was a woman of Bolotoo, mentioning her name, who had died some years before, and who wished him now to die, that he might be near her. He accordingly died in two days. The chief said he suspected this from the dreams he had had at different times, when the figure of a woman came to him in the night. Mr. Mariner was with the sick chief three or four times during his illness, and heard the priest foretell his death, and relate the occasion of it." — *Mariner*.

The following similar case appeared in a newspaper: "Died on Sunday evening, the 14th instant, John Sackeouse, aged twenty-two, a native of the west coast of Greenland. This Esquimau has occupied a considerable share of public attention, and his loss will be very generally felt. He had already rendered important service to the country in the late expedition of discovery, and great expectations were naturally formed of the utility which he would prove on the expedition about to sail for Baffin's Bay. The Admiralty, with great liberality and judgment, had directed the greatest pains to be taken in his further education; and he had been several months in Edinburgh with this view, when he was seized with a violent inflammation in the chest, which carried him off in a few days. He was extremely docile; and, though rather slow in the attainment of knowledge, he was industrious, zealous, and cheerful, and was always grateful for the kindness and attention shown to him. His amiable disposition and simple manners had interested those who had opportunities of knowing him personally, in a way that will not soon be forgotten. To the public, his loss, we fear, is irreparable; to his friends, it is doubly severe. Just before his death, the poor Esquimau said he knew be was going to die; that his father and mother had died in the same way; and that his sister, who was the last of all his relations, had just appeared to him, and called him away." — *Edinburgh Courant*, Feb. 19.

ALL FOR LOVE;

OR,

A SINNER WELL SAVED.

TO CAROLINE BOWLES.

COULD I look forward to a distant day,
With hope of building some elaborate lay,
Then would I wait till worthier strains of mine
Might bear inscribed thy name, O Caroline!
For I would, while my voice is heard on earth,
Bear witness to thy genius and thy worth.
But we have both been taught to feel with fear
How frail the tenure of existence here;
What unforeseen calamities prevent,
Alas, how oft! the best-resolved intent;
And therefore this poor volume I address
To thee, dear friend, and sister Poetess!

ROBERT SOUTHEY.

KESWICK, Feb. 21, 1829.

THE story of the following poem is taken from a "Life of St. Basil," ascribed to his contemporary St. Amphilochius, Bishop of Iconium; a Latin version of which, made by Cardinal

Ursus in the ninth century, is inserted by Rosweyde among the "Lives of the Fathers," in his compilation "Historiæ Eremiticæ." The original had not then been printed; but Rosweyde obtained a copy of it from the Royal Library at Paris. He intimates no suspicion concerning the authenticity of the life, or the truth of this particular legend; observing only, that "hæc narratio apud solum invenitur Amphilochium." It is, indeed, the flower of the work; and, as such, had been culled by some earlier translator than Ursus.

The very learned Dominican, P. François Combefis, published the original, with a version of his own, and endeavored to establish its authenticity in opposition to Baronius, who supposed the life to have been written by some other Amphilochius, not by the Bishop of Iconium. Had Combefis possessed powers of mind equal to his erudition, he might even then have been in some degree prejudiced upon this subject; for, according to Baillet, "il avoit un attachement particulier pour S. Basile." His version is inserted in the "Acta Sanctorum" (Jun. t. ii. pp. 937–57). But the Bollandist Baert brands the life there as apocryphal; and, in his annotations, treats Combefis more rudely, it may be suspected, than he would have done had he not belonged to a rival and hostile order.

I.

A Youth hath entered the Sorcerer's door;
But he dares not lift his eye,
For his knees fail, and his flesh quakes,
And his heart beats audibly.

"Look up, young man!" the Sorcerer said;
"Lay open thy wishes to me!
Or art thou too modest to tell thy tale?
If so, I can tell it thee.

"Thy name is Eleëmon;
Proterius's freedman thou art;
And on Cyra, thy Master's daughter,
Thou hast madly fixed thy heart.

"But fearing (as thou well mayst fear!)
The high-born Maid to woo,
Thou hast tried what secret prayers and vows
And sacrifice might do.

"Thou hast prayed unto all Saints in Heaven,
And to Mary their vaunted Queen;
And little furtherance hast thou found
From them or from her, I ween!

"And thou, I know, the Ancient Gods,
In hope forlorn, hast tried,
If haply Venus might obtain
The maiden for thy bride.

"On Jove and Phœbus thou hast called,
And on Astarte's name,
And on her who still at Ephesus
Retains a faded fame.

"Thy voice to Baal hath been raised;
To Nile's old Deities;
And to all Gods of elder time,
Adored by men in every clime,
When they ruled earth, seas, and skies.

"Their Images are deaf!
Their Oracles are dumb!
And therefore thou, in thy despair,
To Abibas art come.

"Ay, because neither Saints nor Gods
Thy pleasure will fulfil,
Thou comest to me, Eleëmon,
To ask if Satan will!

"I answer thee, 'Yes!' But a faint heart
Can never accomplish its ends:
Put thy trust boldly in him, and be sure
He never forsakes his friends."

While Eleëmon listened,
He shuddered inwardly
At the ugly voice of Abibas,
And the look in his wicked eye.

And he could then almost have given
His fatal purpose o'er;
But his Good Angel had left him
When he entered the Sorcerer's door.

So, in the strength of evil shame,
His mind the young man knit
Into a desperate resolve,
For his bad purpose fit.

"Let thy Master give me what I seek,
O Servant of Satan!" he said,
"As I ask firmly, and for his
Renounce all other aid!

"Time presses. Cyra is content
To bid the world farewell,
And pass her days, a virgin vowed,
Among Emmelia's sisterhood,
The tenant of a cell.

"Thus hath her Father willed, that so
A life of rigor here below
May fit her for the skies,
And Heaven acceptably receive
His costliest sacrifice.

"The admiring people say of this,
That Angels, or that Saints in bliss,
That holy thought inspire;
And she is called a blessèd Maid,
And he a happy Sire.

"Through Cappadocia far and wide
The news hath found its way,
And crowds to Cæsarea flock
To attend the solemn day.

"The robes are ready, rich with gold,
Even like a bridal dress,

Which at the altar she will wear
When self-devoted she stands there
In all her loveliness.

"And that coarse habit, too, which she
Must then put on, is made,
Therein to be for life and death
Unchangeably arrayed.

"This night, this precious night, is ours;
Late, late, I come to you;
But all that must be dared or done,
Prepared to dare and do."

"Thou hast hesitated long!" said Abibas;
"And thou hast done amiss,
In praying to Him whom I name not,
That it never might come to this!

"But thou hast chosen thy part, and here thou art,
And thou shalt have thy desire;
And, though at the eleventh hour
Thou hast come to serve our Prince of Power,
He will give thee in full thine hire.

"These Tablets take;" (he wrote as he spake;)
"My letters, which thou art to bear,
Wherein I shall commend thee
To the Prince of the Powers of the Air.

"Go from the North Gate out, and take
On a Pagan's tomb thy stand;
And, looking to the North, hold up
The Tablets in thy hand; —

"And call the Spirits of the Air,
That they my messenger may bear
To the place whither he would pass,
And there present him to their Prince
In the name of Abibas.

"The passage will be swift and safe;
No danger awaits thee beyond;
Thou wilt only have now to sign and seal,
And hereafter to pay the Bond."

II.

SHUNNING human sight, like a thief in the night,
Eleëmon made no delay,
But went unto a Pagan's tomb
Beside the public way.

Enclosed with barren elms it stood,
There planted when the dead
Within the last abode of man
Had been deposited.

And thrice ten years those barren trees,
Enjoying light and air,
Had grown and flourished, while the dead
In darkness mouldered there.

Long had they overtopped the tomb;
And closed was now that upper room
Where friends were wont to pour,
Upon the honored dust below,
Libations through the floor.

There on that unblest monument
The young man took his stand,
And northward he the tablets held
In his uplifted hand.

A courage not his own he felt,
A wicked fortitude,
Wherewith bad influences unseen
That hour his heart endued.

The rising Moon grew pale in heaven
At that unhappy sight;
And all the blessèd Stars seemed then
To close their twinkling light;
And a shuddering in the elms was heard,
Though winds were still that night.

He called the Spirits of the Air,
He called them in the name

Of Abibas; and at the call
The attendant Spirits came.

A strong hand, which he could not see,
Took his uplifted hand;
He felt a strong arm circle him,
And lift him from his stand; —

A whir of unseen wings he heard
About him everywhere,
Which onward, with a mighty force,
Impelled him through the air.

Fast through the middle sky and far
It hurried him along;
The Hurricane is not so swift,
The Torrent not so strong; —

The Lightning travels not so fast,
The Sunbeams not so far;
And now behind him he hath left
The Moon and every Star.

And still, erect as on the tomb
In impious act he stood,
Is he rapt onward, onward, still
In that fixed attitude.

But, as he from the living world
Approached where Spirits dwell,

His bearers there in thinner air
Were dimly visible; —

Shapeless, and scarce to be descried
In darkness where they flew:
But still, as they advanced, the more
And more distinct they grew.

And when their way fast speeding they
Through their own region went,
Then were they in their substance seen, —
The angelic form, the fiendish mien,
Face, look, and lineament.

Behold where dawns before them now,
Far off, the boreal ray,
Sole daylight of that frozen zone,
The limit of their way!

In that drear realm of outer night,
Like the shadow or the ghost of light,
It moved in the restless skies,
And went and came, like a feeble flame
That flickers before it dies.

There the fallen Seraph reigned supreme
Amid the utter waste;
There, on the everlasting ice,
His dolorous throne was placed.

Son of the Morning! is it then
For this that thou hast given
Thy seat, pre-eminent among
The hierarchies of Heaven?—

As if dominion here could joy
To blasted pride impart,
Or this cold region slake the fire
Of Hell within the heart!

Thither the Evil Angels bear
The youth, and, rendering homage there,
Their service they evince,
And in the name of Abibas
Present him to their Prince.

Just as they seized him when he made
The Sorcerer's mandate known,
In that same act and attitude
They set him before the throne.

The fallen Seraph cast on him
A dark, disdainful look;
And from his raised hand scornfully
The proffered tablets took.

"Ay,—love!" he cried. "It serves me well.
There was the Trojan boy,—
His love brought forth a ten-years' war,
And fired the towers of Troy.

"And when my own Mark Antony
Against young Cæsar strove,
And Rome's whole world was set in arms,
The cause was, — all for love!

"Some for ambition sell themselves;
By avarice some are driven;
Pride, envy, hatred, best will move
Some souls; and some for only love
Renounce their hopes of Heaven.

"Yes, of all human follies, love,
Methinks, hath served me best;
The Apple had done but little for me,
If Eve had not done the rest.

"Well, then, young Amorist, whom love
Hath brought unto this pass,
I am willing to perform the word
Of my servant Abibas.

"Thy Master's daughter shall be thine,
And with her sire's consent;
And not more to thy heart's desire
Than to her own content.

"Yea, more; — I give thee with the girl,
Thine after-days to bless,
Health, wealth, long life, and whatsoe'er
The world calls happiness.

"But, mark me! — on conditions, youth!
No paltering here we know!
Dost thou here, solemnly, this hour,
Thy hope of Heaven forego?

"Dost thou renounce thy baptism,
And bind thyself to me,
My woful portion to partake
Through all eternity?

"No lurking purpose shall avail,
When youth may fail and courage quail,
To cheat me by contrition!
I will have thee written down among
The children of Perdition.

"Remember, I deceive thee not,
Nor have I tempted thee!
Thou comest of thine own accord,
And actest knowingly.

"Dost thou, who now to choose art free,
For ever pledge thyself to me?
As I shall help thee, say!" —
"I do; so help me, Satan!" said
The wilful castaway.

"A resolute answer," quoth the Fiend;
"And now then, Child of Dust,

In further proof of that firm heart,
Thou wilt sign a Bond before we part;
For I take thee not on trust!"

Swift as thought, a scroll and a reed were brought,
And to Eleëmon's breast,
Just where the heart-stroke plays, the point
Of the reed was gently pressed.

It pierced not in, nor touched the skin;
But the sense that it caused was such,
As when an electric pellet of light
Comes forcibly out at a touch; —

A sense no sooner felt than gone,
But, with that short feeling, then
A drop of his heart's blood came forth,
And filled the fatal pen.

And, with that pen accurst, he signed
The execrable scroll,
Whereby he to perdition bound
His miserable soul.

"Eleëmon, Eleëmon!" then said the Demon,
"The girl shall be thine,
By the tie she holds divine,
Till time that tie shall sever;
And by this writing thou art mine,
For ever and ever and ever!"

III.

LOOK at yon silent dwelling now!
A heavenly sight is there,
Where Cyra in her chamber kneels
Before the Cross in prayer.

She is not loath to leave the world;
For she hath been taught with joy
To think that prayer and praise thenceforth
Will be her life's employ.

And thus her mind hath she inclined,
Her pleasure being still
(An only child, and motherless)
To do her Father's will.

The moonlight falls upon her face,
Upraised in fervor meek,
While peaceful tears of piety
Are stealing down her cheek.

That duty done, the harmless Maid
Disposed herself to rest;
No sin, no sorrow, in her soul,
No trouble in her breast.

But when upon the pillow then,
Composed, she laid her head,

She little thought what unseen Powers
Kept watch beside her bed.

A double ward had she that night,
When evil near her drew;
Her own Good Angel guarding her,
And Eleëmon's too.

Their charge it was to keep her safe
From all unholy things;
And o'er her, while she slept, they spread
The shadow of their wings.

So, when an Evil Dream drew nigh,
They barred him from access,
Nor suffered him to reach her with
A breath of sinfulness; —

But with his instigations they
A hallowing influence blent,
And made his fiendish ministry
Subserve to their intent.

Thus while in troubled sleep she lay,
Strange impulses were given,
Emotions earthly and of earth,
With heavenly ones of Heaven.

And now the nightingale hath ceased
Her strain, who all night long

Hath in the garden rosier trilled
A rich and rapturous song.

The storks on roof and dome and tower
Forbear their clattering din,
As now the motions and the sounds
Of daily life begin.

Then as, from dreams that seemed no dreams,
The wondering Maid awoke,
A low, sweet voice was in her ear,
Such as we might expect to hear
If some Good Angel spoke.

According with her dreams, it said,
" So, Cyra, must it be:
The duties of a wedded life
Hath Heaven ordained for thee."

This was no dream full well she knew;
For open-eyed she lay,
Conscious of thought and wakefulness,
And in the light of day;
And twice it spake, if doubt had been,
To do all doubt away.

Alas! but how shall she make known
This late and sudden change?
Or how obtain belief for what
Even to herself is strange?

How will her Father brook a turn
That must to all seem shame?
How bear to think that vulgar tongues
Are busy with her name?—

That she should for a voice — a dream —
Expose herself to be the theme
Of wonder and of scorn;
Public as her intent had been,
And this the appointed morn!

The Nuns even now are all alert;
The altar hath been dressed,
The scissors that should clip her hair
Provided, and the black hood there,
And there the sable vest.

And there the Priests are robing now;
The Singers in their station:
Hark! in the city she can hear
The stir of expectation!

Through every gate the people pour,
And guests on roof and porch and tower
Expectant take their place;
The streets are swarming, and the church
Already fills apace.

Speak, then, she must: her heart she felt
This night had changed its choice;

Nor dared the Maiden disobey —
Nor did she wish to (sooth to say) —
That sweet and welcome voice.

Her Father comes: she studies not
For gloss or for pretence;
The plain, straight course will Cyra take
(Which none without remorse forsake)
Of truth and innocence.

"O Father, hear me patiently!"
The blushing Maiden said:
"I tremble, Father, while I speak,
But surely not for dread.

"If all my wishes have till now
Found favor in thy sight,
And ever to perform thy will
Hath been my best delight,
Why should I fear to tell thee now
The visions of this night?

"I stood in a dream at the altar, —
But it was an earthly Bride;
And Eleëmon, thy freedman,
Was the Bridegroom at my side.

"Thou, Father, gavest me to him
With thy free and full consent;
And — why should I dissemble it? —
Methought I was content.

"Months then and years were crowded
In the course of that busy night:
I clasped a baby to my breast,
And, oh, with what delight!

"Yea, I was fruitful as a vine;
Our Heavenly Parent me and mine
In all things seemed to bless;
Our ways were ways of peace, our paths
Were paths of pleasantness.

"When I taught lisping lips to pray,
The joy it was to me,
O Father, thus to train these plants
For immortality!

"I saw their little winning ways
Their grandsire's love engage:
Methought they were the pride, the joy,
The crown, of his old age.

"When from the Vision I awoke,
A voice was in my ear, —
A waking voice; I heard it twice;
No human tongue was near; —

"No human utterance so could reach
The secret soul, no human speech
So make the soul rejoice:
In hearing it, I felt and knew
It was an Angel's voice!

"And thus, in words distinct, it said,
'So, Cyra, must it be:
The duties of a wedded life
Hath Heaven ordained for thee.'"

Her cheek was like the new-blown rose,
While thus she told her tale:
Proterius listened earnestly,
And, as he heard, grew pale; —

For he, too, in the dreams of night,
At the altar had seemed to stand,
And to Eleëmon, his freedman,
Had given his daughter's hand.

Their offspring, courting his caress,
About his knees had thronged;
A lovely progeny, in whom,
When he was in the silent tomb,
His line should be prolonged.

And he had heard a waking voice,
Which said it so must be,
Pronouncing upon Cyra's name
A holiest eulogy: —

"Her shall her husband praise, and her
Her children blest shall call:
Many daughters have done virtuously,
But thine excelleth them all!"

No marvel if his heart were moved;
The dream he saw was one:
He kissed his trembling child, and said,
"The will of Heaven be done!"

Little did child or sire in this
The work of sorcery fear;
As little did Eleëmon think
That the hand of Heaven was here.

IV.

From house to house, from street to street,
The rapid rumor flies;
Incredulous ears it found, and hands
Are lifted in surprise;
And tongues through all the astonished town
Are busier now than eyes.

"So sudden and so strange a change!
A Freedman, too, the choice!
The shame, — the scandal, — and for what?
A vision and a voice!

"Had she not chosen the strait gate, —
The narrow way, — the holy state, —
The Sanctuary's abode?
Would Heaven call back its votary
To the broad and beaten road?

"To carnal wishes would it turn
The mortified intent?
For this are miracles vouchsafed?
For this are Angels sent?

"A plain collusion, a device
Between the girl and youth!
Good easy man must the Father be,
To take such tale for truth!"

So judged the acrid and the austere,
And they whose evil heart
Inclines them, in whate'er betides,
To take the evil part.

But others, whom a kindlier frame
To better thoughts inclined,
Preserved, amid their wonderment,
An equitable mind.

They would not of Proterius thus
Injuriously misdeem, —
A grave, good man, and with the wise
For wisdom in esteem.

No easy ear or vain belief
Would he to falsehood lend;
Nor ever might light motive him
From well-weighed purpose bend.

And surely on his pious child,
The gentle Cyra, meek and mild,
Could no suspicion rest;
For in this daughter he had been
Above all fathers blest.

As dutiful as beautiful,
Her praise was widely known;
Being one who, as she grew in years,
Had still in goodness grown.

And what though Eleëmon were
A man of lowly birth?
Enough it was if Nature had
Ennobled him with worth.

"This was no doubtful thing," they said,
"For he had in the house been bred,
Nor e'er from thence removed;
But there from childhood had been known
And trusted and approved.

"Such as he was, his qualities
Might to the world excuse
The Maid and Father for their choice,
Without the vision and the voice,
Had they been free to choose.

"But Heaven by miracle had made
Its pleasure manifest;

That manifested will must set
All doubtful thoughts to rest:
Mysterious though they be, the ways
Of Providence are best."

The wondering City thus discoursed:
To Abibas alone
The secret truth, and even to him
But half the truth, was known.

Meantime the Church hath been prepared
For spousal celebration:
The Sisters to their cells retire,
Amazed at such mutation.

The habit and hood of camel's hair,
Which with the sacred scissors there
On the altar were displayed,
Are taken thence, and in their stead
The marriage-rings are laid.

Behold, in garments gay with gold,
For other spousals wrought,
The Maiden from her Father's house
With bridal pomp is brought!

And now before the Holy Door
In the Ante-nave they stand;
The Bride and Bridegroom side by side,
The Paranymphs, in festal pride,
Arranged on either hand.

Then from the Sanctuary the Priests,
With incense burning sweet,
Advance, and at the Holy Door
The Bride and Bridegroom meet.

There to the Bride and Bridegroom they
The marriage-tapers gave;
And to the altar as they go,
With crossway movement to and fro,
The thuribule they wave.

For fruitfulness, and perfect love,
And constant peace, they prayed,
On Eleëmon, the Lord's Servant,
And Cyra, the Lord's Handmaid.

They called upon the Lord to bless
Their spousal celebration,
And sanctify the marriage rite
To both their souls' salvation.

A pause at every prayer they made;
Whereat, with one accord,
The Choristers took up their part,
And sung, in tones that thrilled the heart,
"Have mercy on us, Lord!"

Then with the marriage rings the Priest
Betrothed them each to each,
And, as the sacred pledge was given,
Resumed his awful speech; —

Pronouncing them, before high Heaven,
This hour espoused to be,
Now and for evermore, for time
And for eternity.

This did he in the presence
Of Angels and of men;
And at every pause the Choristers
Intoned their deep "Amen!"

Then to that gracious Lord, the Priest
His supplication made,
Who, as our Sacred Scriptures tell,
Did bring Rebecca to the well
When Abraham's servant prayed.

He called upon that gracious Lord
To stablish with his power
The espousals made between them,
In truth and love, this hour; —

And with his mercy and his word
Their lot, now linked, to bless,
And let his Angel guide them
In the way of righteousness.

With a Christian benediction,
The Priest dismissed them then;
And the Choristers, with louder voice,
Intoned the last "Amen!"

The days of Espousals are over;
And on the Crowning-day,
To the sacred fane the bridal train,
A gay procession, take again
Through thronging streets their way.

Before them, by the Paranymphs,
The coronals are borne,
Composed of all sweet flowers of spring
By virgin hands that morn.

With lighted tapers in array
They enter the Holy Door;
And the Priest with the waving thuribule
Perfumes the way before.

He raised his voice, and called aloud
On Him who from the side
Of our first Father, while he slept,
Formed Eve to be his bride; —

Creating Woman thus for Man
A helpmate meet to be,
For youth and age, for good and ill,
For weal and woe, united still
In strict society, —

Flesh of his flesh; appointing them
One flesh to be, one heart.
Whom God hath joined together,
Them let not man dispart!

And on our Lord he called, by whom
The marriage feast was blest,
When first by miracle he made
His glory manifest.

Then, in the ever-blessèd Name,
Almighty over all,
From the man's Paranymph he took
The marriage coronal; —

And crowning him therewith, in that
Thrice holy Name, he said,
"Eleëmon, the Servant of God, is crowned
For Cyra, the Lord's Handmaid!"

Next, with like action and like words,
Upon her brow he set
Her coronal, intwined wherein
The rose and lily met:
How beautifully they beseemed
Her locks of glossy jet!

Her he for Eleëmon crowned,
The Servant of the Lord:
Alas! how little did that name
With his true state accord!

"Crown them with honor, Lord!" he said,
"With blessings crown the righteous head!

To them let peace be given,
A holy life, a hopeful end,
A heavenly crown in Heaven!"

Still as he made each separate prayer
For blessings that they in life might share,
And for their eternal bliss,
The echoing Choristers replied,
"O Lord! so grant thou this!"

How differently, meantime, before
The altar as they knelt,
While they the sacred rites partake
Which endless matrimony make,
The Bride and Bridegroom felt!

She, who possessed her soul in peace
And thoughtful happiness,
With her whole heart had inly joined
In each devout address.

His lips the while had only moved
In hollow repetition;
For he had steeled himself, like one
Bound over to perdition.

In present joy he wrapped his heart,
And resolutely cast
All other thoughts beside him,
Of the future or the past.

V.

Twelve years have held their quiet course
Since Cyra's nuptial day:
How happily, how rapidly,
Those years have passed away!

Blest in her husband she hath been:
He loved her as sincerely
(Most sinful and unhappy man!)
As he had bought her dearly.

She hath been fruitful as a vine,
And in her children blest;
Sorrow hath not come near her yet,
Nor fears to shake, nor cares to fret,
Nor grief to wound the breast.

And blest alike would her husband be,
Were all things as they seem:
Eleëmon hath every earthly good,
And with every man's esteem.

But, where the accursèd reed had drawn
The heart-blood from his breast,
A small red spot remained
Indelibly impressed.

Nor could he from his heart throw off
The consciousness of his state;

It was there with a dull, uneasy sense,
A coldness and a weight; —

It was there when he lay down at night,
It was there when at morn he rose;
He feels it whatever he does,
It is with him wherever he goes.

No occupation from his mind
That constant sense can keep;
It is present in his waking hours,
It is present in his sleep; —

But still he felt it most,
And with painfulest weight it pressed,
O miserable man!
When he was happiest.

O miserable man,
Who hath all the world to friend,
Yet dares not in prosperity
Remember his latter end!

But happy man, whate'er
His earthly lot may be,
Who looks on Death as the Angel
That shall set his spirit free,
And bear it to its heritage
Of immortality!

In such faith hath Proterius lived;
And strong is that faith, and fresh,
As if obtaining then new power,
When he had reached the awful hour
Appointed for all flesh.

Eleëmon and his daughter
With his latest breath he blest;
And saying to them, "We shall meet
Again before the Mercy-seat!"
Went peacefully to rest.

This is the balm which God
Hath given for every grief;
And Cyra, in her anguish,
Looked heavenward for relief.

But her miserable husband
Heard a voice within him say,
"Eleëmon, Eleëmon,
Thou art sold to the Demon!"
And his heart seemed dying away.

Whole Cæsarea is poured forth
To see the funeral state,
When Proterius is borne to his resting-place
Without the Northern Gate.

Not like a Pagan's is his bier
At doleful midnight borne

By ghastly torchlight, and with wail
Of women hired to mourn.

With tapers in the face of day,
These rites their faithful hope display;
In long procession slow,
With hymns that fortify the heart,
And prayers that soften woe.

In honor of the dead man's rank,
But of his virtues more,
The holy Bishop Basil
Was one the bier who bore.

And with the Bishop side by side,
As nearest to the dead allied,
Was Eleëmon seen:
All marked, but none could read aright,
The trouble in his mien.

"His master's benefits on him
Were well bestowed," they said,
"Whose sorrow now full plainly showed
How well he loved the dead."

They little weened what thoughts in him
The solemn psalm awoke,
Which to all other hearts that hour
Its surest comfort spoke:—

"Gather my Saints together:
In peace let them be laid,
They who with me," thus saith the Lord,
"Their covenant have made!"

What pangs to Eleëmon then,
O wretchedest of wretched men,
That psalmody conveyed!
For conscience told him that he, too,
A covenant had made.

And when he would have closed his ears
Against the unwelcome word,
Then from some elms beside the way
A Raven's croak was heard.

To him it seemed a hollow voice
That warned him of his doom;
For the tree whereon the Raven sate
Grew over the Pagan's tomb.

VI.

When weariness would let her
No longer pray and weep,
And midnight long was past,
Then Cyra fell asleep.

Into that wretched sleep she sunk
Which only sorrow knows,
Wherein the exhausted body rests,
But the heart hath no repose.

Of her Father she was dreaming,
Still aware that he was dead,
When, in the visions of the night,
He stood beside her bed.

Crowned and in robes of light he came:
She saw he had found grace;
And yet there seemed to be
A trouble in his face.

The eye and look were still the same
That she from her cradle knew:
And he put forth his hand, and blest her,
As he had been wont to do.

But then the smile benign
Of love forsook his face,
And a sorrowful displeasure
Came darkly in its place; —

And he cast on Eleëmon
A melancholy eye,
And sternly said, "I bless thee not, —
Bondsman! thou knowest why!"

Again to Cyra then he turned, —
"Let not thy husband rest
Till he hath washed away with tears
The red spot from his breast!

"Hold fast thy hope, and Heaven will not
Forsake thee in thine hour:
Good Angels will be near thee,
And evil ones shall fear thee,
And Faith will give thee power."

Perturbed, yet comforted, she woke;
For in her waking ear
The words were heard which promised her
A strength above all fear.

An odor, that refreshed no less
Her spirit with its blessedness
Than her corporeal frame,
Was breathed around, and she surely found
That from Paradise it came.

And, though the form revered was gone,
A clear, unearthly light
Remained, encompassing the bed,
When all around was night.

It narrowed as she gazed;
And soon she saw it rest,
Concentred, like an eye of light,
Upon her husband's breast.

Not doubting now the presence
Of some good-presiding Power,
Collectedness as well as strength
Was given her in this hour.

And, rising half, the while in deep
But troubled sleep he lay,
She drew the covering from his breast
With cautious hand away.

The small, round, blood-red mark she saw:
Eleëmon felt her not;
But in his sleep he groaned, and cried,
"Out, out, accursèd spot!"

The darkness of surrounding night
Closed then upon that eye of light:
She waited for the break
Of day, and lay the while in prayer
For that poor sinner's sake, —

In fearful, miserable prayer:
But, while she prayed, the load of care,
Less heavily bore on her heart,
And light was given, enabling her
To choose her difficult part; —

And she drew, as comfortable texts
Unto her thoughts recurred,
Refreshment from the living well
Of God's unerring word.

But, when the earliest dawn appeared,
Herself in haste she arrayed,
And watched his waking patiently,
And still as she watched she prayed ;
And, when Eleëmon had risen,
She spake to him, and said, —

"We have been visited this night ;
My Father's Ghost I have seen ;
I heard his voice, — an awful voice ! —
And so hast thou, I ween ! "

Eleëmon was pale when he awoke ;
But paler then he grew,
And over his whole countenance
There came a deathlike hue.

Still he controlled himself, and sought
Her question to beguile ;
And forcing, while he answered her,
A faint and hollow smile, —

"Cyra," he said, "thy thoughts, possessed
With one too painful theme,
Their own imaginations
For reality misdeem :
Let not my dearest, best beloved,
Be troubled for a Dream ! "

"O Eleëmon ! " she replied,
"Dissemble not with me thus :

Ill it becomes me to forget
What Dreams have been to us!

"'Think'st thou there can be peace for me,
Near to me as thou art,
While some unknown and fearful sin
Is festering at thy heart?

"Eleëmon, Eleëmon!
I may not let thee rest,
Till thou hast washed away with tears
The red spot from thy breast!

"Thus to conceal thy crime from me,
It is no tenderness!
The worst is better known than feared:
Whatever it be, confess;
And the Merciful will cleanse thee
From all unrighteousness!"

Like an aspen-leaf he trembled;
And his imploring eye
Bespake compassion, ere his lips
Could utter their dreaded reply.

"O dearly loved, as dearly bought!
My sin and punishment I had thought
To bear through life alone:
Too much the Vision hath revealed,
And all must now be known!

"On thee, methinks, and only thee,
Dare I for pity call;
Abhor me not, renounce me not,
My life, my love, my all!

"And, Cyra, sure, if ever cause
Might be a sinner's plea,
'Twould be for that lost wretch who sold
His hope of Heaven for thee!

"Thou seest a miserable man
Given over to despair,
Who has bound himself, by his act and deed,
To the Prince of the Powers of the Air."

She seized him by the arm,
And hurrying him into the street,
"Come with me to the Church," she cried,
"And to Basil the Bishop's feet!"

VII.

Public must be the sinner's shame,
As heinous his offence;
So Basil said, when he ordained
His form of penitence.

And never had such dismay been felt
Through that astonished town,

As when, at morn, the Crier went
Proclaiming up and down, —

"The miserable sinner, Eleëmon,
Who for love hath sold himself to the Demon,
His guilt before God and man declares,
And beseeches all good Christians
To aid him with their prayers."

Many were the hearts compassionate
Whom that woful petition moved;
For he had borne his fortune meekly,
And therefore was well beloved.

Open his hand had been,
And liberal of its store;
And the prayers of the needy arose,
Who had daily been fed at his door.

They, too, whom Cyra's secret aid
Relieved from pressing cares,
In this her day of wretchedness
Repaid her with their prayers.

And from many a gentle bosom
Supplications for mercy were sent,
If haply they might aid
The wretched penitent.

Sorely such aid he needed then!
Basil himself, of living men

The powerfulest in prayer,
For pity, rather than in hope,
Had bidden him not despair.

So hard a thing for him it seemed
To wrest from Satan's hand
The fatal Bond, which, while retained,
Must against him in judgment stand.

"Dost thou believe," he said, "that Grace
Itself can reach this grief?"
With a feeble voice, and a woful eye,
"Lord, I believe!" was the sinner's reply:
"Help thou mine unbelief!"

The Bishop then crossed him on the brow,
And crossed him on the breast;
And told him, if he did his part
With true remorse and faithful heart,
God's mercy might do the rest.

"Alone in the holy Relic-room
Must thou pass day and night,
And wage with thy ghostly enemies
A more than mortal fight.

"The trial may be long, and the struggle strong;
Yet be not thou dismayed;
For thou mayest count on Saints in Heaven,
And on earthly prayers, for aid.

"And in thy mind this scripture bear
With steadfast faithfulness, whate'er
To appall thee may arrive, —
'When the wicked man turneth away from his sin,
He shall save his soul alive!'

"Take courage as thou lookest around
On the relics of the blest;
And, night and day, continue to pray,
Until thy tears have washed away
The stigma from thy breast!"

"Let me be with him!" Cyra cried:
"If thou mayest not be there,
In this sore trial I at least
My faithful part may bear.

"My presence may some comfort prove,
Yea, haply some defence:
O Father, in myself I feel
The strength of innocence!"

"Nay, Daughter, nay; it must not be!
Though dutiful this desire:
He may by Heaven's good grace be saved,
But only as if by fire.

"Sights which should never meet thine eye
Before him may appear,

And fiendish voices proffer words
Which should never assail thy ear:
Alone must he this trance sustain;
Keep thou thy vigils here!"

He led him to the Relic-room;
Alone he left him there;
And Cyra with the Nuns remained
To pass her time in prayer.

Alone was Eleëmon left
For mercy on Heaven to call:
Deep and unceasing were his prayers,
But not a tear would fall.

His lips were parched, his head was hot,
His eyeballs throbbed with heat;
And in that utter silence
He could hear his temples beat.

But cold his feet, and cold his hands;
And at his heart there lay
An icy coldness unrelieved,
While he prayed the livelong day.

A long, long day! It passed away
In dreadful expectation;
Yet free throughout the day was he
From outward molestation.

Nor sight appeared, nor voice was heard,
Though every moment both he feared:
The Spirits of the Air
Were busy the while in infusing
Suggestions of despair.

And he in strong endeavor still
Against them strove with earnest will:
Heart-piercing was his cry,
Heart-breathed his groaning; but it seemed
That the source of tears was dry.

And now had evening closed:
The dim lamp-light alone
On the stone cross, and the marble walls,
And the shrines of the Martyrs, shone.

Before the Cross Eleëmon lay;
His knees were on the ground:
Courage enough to touch the Cross
Itself, he had not found.

But on the steps of the pedestal
His lifted hands were laid;
And in that lowliest attitude
The suffering sinner prayed.

A strong temptation of the Fiend,
Which bade him despair and die,

He with the aid of Scripture
Had faithfully put by;
And then, as with a dawning hope,
He raised this contrite cry: —

"Oh that mine eyes were fountains!
If the good grace of Heaven
Would give me tears, methinks I then
Might hope to be forgiven!"

To that meek prayer a short, loud laugh
From fiendish lips replied:
Close at his ear he felt it,
And it sounded on every side.

From the four walls and the vaulted roof
A shout of mockery rung;
And the echoing ground repeated the sound,
Which pealed above and below and around,
From many a fiendish tongue.

The lamps went out at that hideous shout;
But darkness had there no place,
For the room was filled with a lurid light
That came from a Demon's face.

A dreadful face it was, — too well
By Eleëmon known!
Alas! he had seen it when he stood
Before the dolorous Throne.

"Eleëmon! Eleëmon!"
Sternly said the Demon,
"How have I merited this?
I kept my covenant with thee,
And placed thee in worldly bliss!

"And still thou mightest have had,
Thine after-days to bless,
Health, wealth, long life, and whatsoe'er
The World calls happiness.

"Fool, to forego thine earthly joys,
Who hast no hope beyond!
For judgment must be given for me,
When I sue thee upon the Bond.

"Remember, I deceived thee not;
Nor had I tempted thee:
Thou camest of thine own accord,
And didst act knowingly!

"I told thee thou mightst vainly think
To cheat me by contrition,
When thou wert written down among
The Children of Perdition!

"'So help me, Satan!' were thy words
When thou didst this allow:
I helped thee, Eleëmon, then, —
And I will have thee now!"

At the words of the Fiend, from the floor
Eleëmon in agony sprung;
Up the steps of the pedestal he ran,
And to the Cross he clung.

And then it seemed as if he drew,
While he clasped the senseless stone,
A strength he had not felt till then,
A hope he had not known.

So, when the Demon ceased,
He answered him not a word;
But, looking upward, he
His faithful prayer preferred: —

"All, all, to Thee, my Lord
And Saviour, I confess!
And I know that Thou canst cleanse me
From all unrighteousness!

"I have turned away from my sin
In Thee do I put my trust:
To such Thou hast promised forgiveness;
And Thou art faithful and just!"

With that the Demon disappeared;
The lamps resumed their light;
Nor voice nor vision more
Disturbed him through the night.

He stirred not from his station,
But there stood fixed in prayer;
And, when Basil the Bishop entered
At morn, he found him there.

VIII.

WELL might the Bishop see what he
Had undergone that night:
Remorse and agony of mind
Had made his dark hair white.

So should the inner change, he weened,
With the outward sign accord;
And holy Basil crossed himself,
And blest our gracious Lord.

"Well hast thou done," he said, "my son,
And faithfully fought the fight;
So shall this day complete, I trust,
The victory of the night.

"I feared that forty days and nights
Too little all might be;
But great and strange hath been the change
One night hath wrought in thee."

"O Father! Father!" he replied,
"And hath it been but one?
An endless time it seemed to me!
I almost thought Eternity
With me had been begun.

"And surely this poor flesh and blood
Such terrors could not have withstood,
If grace had not been given;
But, when I clasped the blessèd Cross,
I then had help from Heaven.

"The coldness from my heart is gone,
But still the weight is there;
And thoughts, which I abhor, will come
And tempt me to despair.

"Those thoughts I constantly repel;
And all, methinks, might yet be well,
Could I but weep once more,
And with true tears of penitence
My dreadful state deplore.

"Tears are denied; their source is dried!
And must it still be so?
O Thou, who from a rock didst make
The living waters flow!—

"A broken and a bleeding heart
This hour I offer Thee;

And, when Thou seest good, my tears
Shall then again be free!"

A knocking at the door was heard
As he ended this reply:
Hearing that unexpected sound,
The Bishop turned his eye;
And his venerable Mother,
Emmelia, the Abbess, drew nigh.

"We have not ceased this mournful night,"
Said she, "on Heaven to call;
And our afflicted Cyra
Hath edified us all.

"More fervent prayers from suffering heart,
I ween, have ne'er been sent;
And now she asks, as some relief
In this her overwhelming grief,
To see the penitent.

"So earnestly she asked, that I
Her wish would not defer;
And I have brought her to the door:
Forgive me, Son, if I err."

"Hard were I did I not consent
To thy compassionate intent,
O Mother!" he replied;
And, raising then his voice, "Come in,
Thou innocent!" he cried.

That welcome word when Cyra heard,
With a sad pace and slow,
Forward she came, like one whose heart
Was overcharged with woe.

Her face was pale, — long illness would
Have changed those features less;
And long-continued tears had dimmed
Her eyes with heaviness.

Her husband's words had reached her ear
When at the door she stood:
"Thou hast prayed in vain for tears," she said,
"While I have poured a flood!

"Mine flow, and they will flow; they must;
They cannot be repressed!
And oh that they might wash away
The stigma from thy breast!

"Oh that these tears might cleanse that spot, —
Tears which I cannot check!"
Profusely weeping as she spake,
She fell upon his neck.

He clasped the mourner close, and in
That passionate embrace,
In grief for her, almost forgot
His own tremendous case.

Warm as they fell, he felt her tears;
And in true sympathy,
So gracious Heaven permitted then,
His own to flow were free.

And then the weight was taken off,
Which at his heart had pressed;—
O mercy! and the crimson spot
Hath vanished from his breast!

At that most happy sight,
The four, with one accord,
Fell on their knees, and blest
The mercy of the Lord.

"What then! before the strife is done,
Would ye of victory boast?"
Said a Voice above: "they reckon too soon
Who reckon without their host!"

"Mine is he by a Bond
Which holds him fast in law:
I drew it myself for certainty;
And sharper than me must the Lawyer be
Who in it can find a flaw!

"Before the Congregation,
And in the face of day,
Whoever may pray, and whoever gainsay,

I will challenge him for my Bondsman,
And carry him quick away!"

"Ha, Satan! dost thou in thy pride,"
With righteous anger Basil cried,
"Defy the force of prayer?
In the face of the Church wilt thou brave it?
Why, then, we will meet thee there!

"There mayest thou set forth thy right,
With all thy might, before the sight
Of all the Congregation;
And they that hour shall see the power
Of the Lord unto salvation!"

"A challenge fair! We meet, then, there!"
Rejoined the Prince of the Powers of the Air;
"The Bondsman is mine by right:
Let the whole city come at thy call,
And great and small: in face of them all,
I will have him in thy despite!"

So, having said, he tarried not
To hear the Saint's reply:
"Beneath the sign which Constantine,"
Said Basil, "beheld in the sky,
We strive, and have our strength therein,
Therein our victory!"

IX.

The Church is filled, so great the faith
That City in its Bishop hath;
And now the Congregation
Are waiting there in trembling prayer
And terrible expectation.

Emmelia and her sisterhood
Have taken there their seat;
And Choristers and Monks and Priests
And Psalmists there, and Exorcists,
Are stationed in order meet.

In sackcloth clad, with ashes strewn
Upon his whiter hair,
Before the steps of the altar,
His feet for penance bare,
Eleëmon stands, a spectacle
For men and Angels there.

Beside him Cyra stood, in weal
Or woe, in good or ill,
Not to be severed from his side,
His faithful helpmate still.

Dishevelled were her raven locks,
As one in mourner's guise;
And pale she was, but faith and hope
Had now relumed her eyes.

At the altar Basil took his stand:
He held the Gospel in his hand;
And in his ardent eye
Sure trust was seen, and conscious power,
And strength for victory.

At his command, the Chorister
Enounced the Prophet's song, —
"To God our Saviour mercies
And forgivenesses belong."

Ten thousand voices joined to raise
The holy hymn on high,
And hearts were thrilled and eyes were filled
By that full harmony.

And when they ceased, and Basil's hand
A warning signal gave,
The whole huge multitude was hushed
In a stillness like that of the grave.

The Sun was high in a bright-blue sky;
But a chill came over the crowd,
And the Church was suddenly darkened,
As if by a passing cloud.

A sound as of a tempest rose,
Though the day was calm and clear:
Intrepid must the heart have been
Which did not then feel fear.

In the sound of the storm came the dreadful Form:
The Church then darkened more;
And He was seen erect on the screen
Over the Holy Door.

Daylight had sickened at his sight;
And the gloomy Presence threw
A shade profound over all around,
Like a cheerless twilight hue.

"I come hither," said the Demon,
"For my Bondsman Eleëmon!
Mine is he, body and soul:
See, all men!" and with that on high
He held the open scroll.

The fatal signature appeared,
To all the multitude,
Distinct as when the accursèd pen
Had traced it with fresh blood.
"See, all men!" Satan cried again,
And then his claim pursued.

"I ask for justice. I prefer
An equitable suit!
I appeal to the Law; and the case
Admitteth of no dispute.

"If there be justice here,
If Law have place in Heaven,

Award upon this Bond
Must then for me be given.

"What to my rightful claim,
Basil, canst thou gainsay,
That I should not seize the Bondsman,
And carry him quick away?

"The writing is confessed; —
No plea against it shown; —
The forfeiture is mine;
And now I take my own!"

"Hold, there!" cried Basil, with a voice
That arrested him on his way,
When from the screen he would have swooped
To pounce upon his prey; —

"Hold, there, I say! Thou canst not sue
Upon this Bond by law!
A sorry legalist were he
Who could not, in thy boasted plea,
Detect its fatal flaw.

"The Deed is null, for it was framed
With fraudulent intent;
A thing unlawful in itself;
A wicked instrument, —
Not to be pleaded in the Courts. —
Sir Fiend, thy cause is shent!

"This were enough; but, more than this,
A maxim, as thou knowest, it is,
Whereof all Laws partake,
That no one may of his own wrong
His own advantage make.

"The man, thou sayest, thy Bondsman is:
Mark, now, how stands the fact!
Thou hast allowed, nay, aided him,
As a Freedman, to contract
A marriage with this Christian woman here,
And by a public act.

"That act being publicly performed
With thy full cognizance,
Claim to him as thy Bondsman thou
Canst never more advance; —

"For when they solemnly were then
United, in sight of Angels and men,
The matrimonial band
Gave to the wife a right in him;
And we on this might stand.

"Thy claim upon the man was by
Thy silence then forsaken;
A marriage thus by thee procured,
May not by thee be shaken;
And thou, O Satan! as thou seest,
In thine own snare art taken!"

So Basil said, and paused awhile;
The Arch-fiend answered not;
But he heaved in vexation
A sulphurous sigh for the Bishop's vocation,
And thus to himself he thought: —

"The Law thy calling ought to have been,
With thy wit so ready, and tongue so free!
To prove by reason, in reason's despite,
That right is wrong, and wrong is right,
And white is black, and black is white, —
What a loss have I had in thee!"

"I rest not here," the Saint pursued;
"Though thou in this mayest see
That in the meshes of thine own net
I could entangle thee!

"Fiend! thou thyself didst bring about
The spousal celebration,
Which linked them by the nuptial tie
For both their souls' salvation.

"Thou sufferedst them before high Heaven
With solemn rites espoused to be,
Then and for evermore, for time
And for eternity.

"That tie holds good; those rites
Will reach their whole intent;

And thou of his salvation wert
Thyself the instrument.

"And now, methinks, thou seest in this
A higher power than thine,
And that thy ways were overruled
To work the will divine!"

With rising energy he spake,
And more majestic look,
And with authoritative hand
Held forth the Sacred Book.

Then with a voice of power he said,
"The Bond is null and void!
It is nullified, as thou knowest well,
By a Covenant whose strength by Hell
Can never be destroyed! —

"The Covenant of grace,
That greatest work of Heaven,
Which whoso claims in perfect faith,
His sins shall be forgiven.

"Were they as scarlet red,
They should be white as wool:
This is the All-mighty's Covenant,
Who is All-merciful!

"His Minister am I!
In his All-mighty name

To this repentant sinner
God's pardon I proclaim!

"In token that against his soul
The sin shall no longer stand,
The writing is effaced, which there
Thou holdest in thy hand!

"Angels that are in bliss above
This triumph of Redeeming Love
Will witness, and rejoice;
And ye shall now in thunder hear
Heaven's ratifying voice!"

A peal of thunder shook the pile;
The Church was filled with light;
And, when the flash was past, the Fiend
Had vanished from their sight.

He fled as he came, but in anger and shame;
The pardon was complete;
And the impious scroll was dropped, a blank,
At Eleëmon's feet.

NOTES TO ALL FOR LOVE.

There, on the everlasting ice,
His dolorous throne was placed. — II. p. 142.

It was the north of heaven that Lucifer, according to grave authors, attempted to take by storm. "En aver criado Dios con tanta hermosura el cielo y la tierra, quedo ordenada su celestial Corte de divinas Hierarchias; mas reynò tanto la ingratitud en uno de los Cortesanos, viendose tan lindo y bello, y en mas eminente lugar que los demas (segun Theodoreto), que quiso emparejar con el Altissimo, y subir al Aquilon, formando para esto una quadrilla de sus confidentes y parciales."

With this sentence, Fr. Marco de Guadalajara y Xaviera begins his account of the "Memorable Expulsion, y justissimo destierro de los Moriscos de España."

The marriage. — IV. p. 157.

The description of the marriage service is taken from Dr. King's work upon the "Rites and Ceremonies of the Greek Church in Russia." "In all the offices of the Greek church," he says, "there is not perhaps a more curious service than this of matrimony, nor any which carries more genuine marks of antiquity; as from the bare perusal of it may be seen, at one view, most of the ceremonies which antiquarians have taken great pains to ascertain." It agrees very closely with the ritual given by Martene, "De Antiquis Ecclesiæ Ritibus," t. ii. pp. 890–98.

In these ceremonies, —

"The which do endless matrimony make," —

the parties are betrothed to each other "for their salvation," — "now and for ever, even unto ages of ages."

The Ante-nave. — IV. p. 157.

The Πρόναος.

The coronals, . . .
Composed of all sweet flowers. — IV. p. 160.

" Formerly these crowns were garlands made of flowers or shrubs; but now there are generally in all churches crowns of silver, or other metals, kept for that purpose." — *Dr. King's Rites*, &c., p. 232.

" A certain crown of flowers used in marriage," says the excellent Bishop Heber (writing from the Carnatic), " has been denounced to me as a device of Satan! And a gentleman has just written to complain that the Danish government of Tranquebar will not allow him to excommunicate some young persons for wearing masks, and acting, as it appears, in a Christmas mummery, or at least in some private rustic theatricals. If this be heathenish, Heaven help the wicked! But I hope you will not suspect that I shall lend any countenance to this kind of ecclesiastical tyranny, or consent to men's consciences being burdened with restrictions so foreign to the cheerful spirit of the gospel." — vol. iii. p. 446.

Basil, of living men
The powerfulest in prayer. — VII. pp. 174–5.

The most remarkable instance of St. Basil's power in prayer is to be found, not in either of his lives, the veracious or the apocryphal one, but in a very curious account of the opinions held by the Armenian Christians, as drawn up for the information of Pope Benedict XII., and inserted by Domenico Bernino in his " Historia di tutte l'Heresie " (Secolo xiv. cap. iv. t. iii. pp. 508–36). It is there related, that on the sixth day of the creation, when the rebellious angels fell from heaven through that opening in the firmament which the Armenians call Arocea, and we the Galaxy, one unlucky angel, who had no participation in their sin, but seems to have been caught in the crowd, fell with them; and many others would in like manner have fallen by no fault of their own, if the Lord had not said unto them, "Pax vobis." But this unfortunate angel was not restored till he obtained, it is not said how, the prayers of St. Basil: his condition meantime, from the sixth day of the creation to the fourth century of the Christian era, must have been even more uncomfortable than that of Klopstock's repentant Devil. — p. 512, § 16.

Eleëmon's penance. — VII. p. 175.

In the legend, the penitent is left forty days and nights to contend with the Powers of Darkness in the Relic-chamber.*

The penances which Indian fanatics voluntarily undertake and perform would be deemed impossible in Europe, if they had not been witnessed by so many persons of unquestionable authority. The penances which the Bramins enjoin are probably more severe than they would otherwise be, on this account, lest they should seem trifling in the eyes of a people accustomed to such exhibitions.

The lamps went out. — VII. p. 179.

There is the authority of a holy man, in the romance of "Merlin," — which is as good authority for such a fact as any thing in the Acta Sanctorum, — that the Devil, like other wild beasts who prowl about seeking what they may devour, is afraid of a light. The holy man's advice to a pious damsel is never to lie down in the dark: "Garde que là où tu coucheras il y ait tousjours clarté, car le Diable haït toutes cleres choses; ni ne vient pas voulontiers où il y a clarté." — vol. i. f. 4.

And white is black, and black is white. — IX. p. 193.

Satan might have been reconciled to St. Basil's profession, if he had understood, by his faculty of second-sight, that this, which it is sometimes the business of a lawyer to prove, would one day be the duty of the Romanists *to believe*, if their church were to tell them so. No less a personage than St. Ignatius

Loyola has asserted this. In his "Exercitia Spiritualia," the 13th of the Rules which are laid down *ad sentiendum cum Ecclesiâ* is in these words: —

"Denique, ut ipsi Ecclesiæ Catholicæ omnino unanimes, conformesque simus, *si quid, quod oculis nostris apparet album, nigrum illa esse definierit, debemus itidem, quod nigrum sit, pronuntiare.* Indubitate namque credendum est, eumdem esse Domini nostri Jesu Christi, et Ecclesiæ orthodoxæ, sponsæ ejus, spiritum, per quem gubernamur ac dirigimur ad salutem; neque alium esse Deum, qui olim tradidit Decalogi præcepta, et qui nunc temporis Ecclesiam hierarchicam instruit atque regit." — p. 141. Antwerpiæ, 1635.

Such is the implicit obedience enjoined in those "Spiritual Exercises," of which Pope Paul III. said in his brief, *Sub annulo Piscatoris*, "Omnia et singula in eis contenta, ex certâ scientiâ nostrâ, approbamus, collaudamus, ac præsentis scripti patrocinio communimus." The Romanists are to believe that black is white, if the Roman church tells them so: morally and politically it has often told them so; and *they have believed and acted accordingly.*

THE

PILGRIM TO COMPOSTELLA;

BEING THE

LEGEND OF A COCK AND A HEN, TO THE HONOR AND GLORY OF SANTIAGO.

A CHRISTMAS TALE.

Res similis fictæ; sed quid mihi fingere prodest.
OVID, Met. xiii. v. 935.

Hear also no lean story of theirs! — LIGHTFOOT.

THE legend (for a genuine legend it is) which has been made the subject of the ensuing ballad is related by Bishop Patrick in his "Parable of the Pilgrim" (ch. xxxv. pp. 430–34). Udal ap Rhys relates it in his "Tour through Spain and Portugal" (pp. 35–38). Both these writers refer to Lucius Marineus Siculus as their authority. And it is told also in the "Journal du Voyage d'Espagne" (Paris, 1669), by a *Conseiller* who was attached to the French embassy in that country (p. 18).

The story may likewise be found in the "Acta Sanctorum." A duplicate of the principal miracle occurs in the third volume, for the month of May (*die* 12â, p. 171), and is there ascribed to S. Domingo de la Calzada; the author, Luiz de la Vega, contending that both relations are to be received as true, the Bollandist (Henschenius) contrariwise opining that they are distinct miracles, but leaving the reader nevertheless to determine freely for himself "utrum id malit, an vero credere velit, unicum dumtaxat esse quod sub quadam circumstantiarum varietate refertur ut geminum."

In the sixth volume of the same work, for the month of

July (*die* 25â), the legend of the Pilgrim is twice told, — once (p. 45) as occurring to a native of Utrecht (Cæsarius Heisterbachensis is the authority); once as having befallen a German at Thoulouse (p. 50). The latter story is in the collection of Santiago's miracles, which Pope Calixtus II. is said to have compiled.

PRELUDE.

"Tell us a story, old Robin Gray!
This merry Christmas time:
We are all in our glory; so tell us a story,
Either in prose or in rhyme.

"Open your budget, old Robin Gray!
We very well know it is full:
Come! out with a murder, a Goblin, a Ghost,
Or a tale of a Cock and a Bull!"

"I have no tale of a Cock and a Bull,
My good little women and men;
But 'twill do as well, perhaps, if I tell
A tale of a Cock and a Hen."

INTRODUCTION.

You have all of you heard of St. James for Spain,
As one of the Champions Seven,
Who, having been good Knights on Earth,
Became Hermits, and Saints in Heaven.

Their history once was in good repute,
And so it ought to be still:
Little friends, I dare say you have read it;
And if not, why, I hope you will.

Of this St. James that book proclaims
Great actions manifold;
But more amazing are the things
Which of him in Spain are told; —

How once a ship, of marble made,
Came sailing o'er the sea,
Wherein his headless corpse was laid,
Perfumed with sanctity; —

And how, though then he had no head,
He afterwards had two,
Which both worked miracles so well,
That it was not possible to tell
The false one from the true; * —

---

* Whereby, my little friends, we see
That an original may sometimes be
No better than its fac-simile:
A useful truth, I trow,
Which picture-buyers won't believe,
But which picture-dealers know.

Young Connoisseurs who will be,
Remember I say this —
For your benefit hereafter —
In a parenthesis.

And, not to interrupt
The order of narration,
This warning shall be printed
By way of annotation.

And how he used to fight the Moors
Upon a milk-white charger:
Large tales of him the Spaniards tell;
Munchausen tells no larger.

But in their cause, of latter years,
He has not been so hearty;
For that he never struck a stroke is plain,
When our Duke, in many a hard campaign,
Beat the French armies out of Spain,
And conquered Bonapartè.

Yet still they worship him in Spain,
And believe in him with might and main;
Santiago there they call him;
And, if any one there should doubt these tales,
They've an Inquisition to maul him.

At Compostella, in his Church,
His body and one head
Have been, for some eight hundred years,
By Pilgrims visited.

Old scores might there be clean rubbed off;
And tickets there were given
To clear all toll-gates on the way
Between the Churchyard and Heaven.

Some went for payment of a vow
In time of trouble made;

And some, who found that pilgrimage
Was a pleasant sort of trade; —

And some, I trow, because it was
Believed, as well as said,
That all, who in their mortal stage
Did not perform this pilgrimage,
Must make it when they were dead; —

Some upon penance for their sins,
In person, or by attorney;
And some who were or had been sick;
And some who thought to cheat Old Nick;
And some who liked the journey; —

Which well they might when ways were safe;
And therefore rich and poor
Went in that age on pilgrimage,
As folks now make a tour.

The poor with scrip, the rich with purse,
They took their chance for better, for worse,
From many a foreign land,
With a scallop-shell in the hat for badge,
And a Pilgrim's staff in hand.

Something there is, the which to leave
Untold would not be well,
Relating to the Pilgrim's staff,
And to the scallop-shell.

For the scallop shows, in a coat-of-arms,
That of the bearer's line
Some one, in former days, hath been
To Santiago's shrine.

And the staff was bored and drilled for those
Who on a flute could play;
And thus the merry Pilgrim had
His music on the way.

THE LEGEND.

PART I.

ONCE on a time, three Pilgrims true,
Being Father and Mother and Son,
For pure devotion to the Saint,
This pilgrimage begun.

Their names, little friends, I am sorry to say,
In none of my books can I find:
But the son, if you please, we'll call Pierre;
What the parents were called, never mind.

From France they came, in which fair land
They were people of good renown;
And they took up their lodging one night on the way
In La Calzada town.

Now, if poor Pilgrims they had been,
And had lodged in the Hospice instead of the Inn,
My good little women and men,
Why, then you never would have heard
This tale of the Cock and the Hen.

For the Innkeepers they had a daughter,
Sad to say, who was just such another
As Potiphar's daughter, I think, would have been,
If she followed the ways of her mother.

This wicked woman to our Pierre
Behaved like Potiphar's wife;
And, because she failed to win his love,
She resolved to take his life.

So she packed up a silver cup
In his wallet privily;
And then, as soon as they were gone,
She raised a hue and cry.

The Pilgrims were overtaken;
The people gathered round;
Their wallets were searched, and in Pierre's
The silver cup was found.

They dragged him before the Alcade;
A hasty Judge was he:
"The theft," he said, "was plain and proved;
And hanged the thief must be."

So to the gallows our poor Pierre
Was hurried instantly.

If I should now relate
The piteous lamentation
Which for their son these parents made,
My little friends, I am afraid
You'd weep at the relation.

But Pierre in Santiago still
His constant faith professed :
When to the gallows he was led,
" 'Twas a short way to Heaven," he said,
" Though not the pleasantest."

And from their pilgrimage he charged
His parents not to cease ;
Saying, that, unless they promised this,
He could not be hanged in peace.

They promised it with heavy hearts :
Pierre then, therewith content,
Was hanged ; and they upon their way
To Compostella went.

PART II.

FOUR weeks they travelled painfully :
They paid their vows, and then

To La Calzada's fatal town
Did they come back again.

The Mother would not be withheld,
But go she must to see
Where her poor Pierre was left to hang
Upon the gallows-tree.

Oh tale most marvellous to hear,
Most marvellous to tell!
Eight weeks had he been hanging there,
And yet was alive and well!

"Mother," said he, "I am glad you're returned:
It is time I should now be released;
Though I cannot complain that I'm tired,
And my neck does not ache in the least.

"The Sun has not scorched me by day;
The Moon has not chilled me by night;
And the winds have but helped me to swing,
As if in a dream of delight.

"Go you to the Alcade,
That hasty Judge unjust:
Tell him Santiago has saved me,
And take me down he must!"

Now, you must know the Alcade,
Not thinking himself a great sinner,

Just then at table had sate down,
About to begin his dinner.

His knife was raised to carve
The dish before him then:
Two roasted Fowls were laid therein;
That very morning they had been
A Cock and his faithful Hen.

In came the Mother, wild with joy:
"A miracle!" she cried;
But that most hasty Judge unjust
Repelled her in his pride.

"Think not," quoth he, "to tales like this
That I should give belief!
Santiago never would bestow
His miracles, full well I know,
On a Frenchman and a thief."

And pointing to the Fowls, o'er which
He held his ready knife,
"As easily might I believe
These birds should come to life!"

The good Saint would not let him thus
The Mother's true tale withstand;
So up rose the Fowls in the dish,
And down dropped the knife from his hand.

The Cock would have crowed, if he could;
To cackle, the Hen had a wish;
And they both slipped about in the gravy,
Before they got out of the dish.

And when each would have opened its eyes,
For the purpose of looking about them,
They saw they had no eyes to open,
And that there was no seeing without them.

All this was to them a great wonder;
They staggered and reeled on the table;
And either to guess where they were,
Or what was their plight, or how they came there,
Alas! they were wholly unable;—

Because, you must know, that that morning—
A thing which they thought very hard—
The Cook had cut off their heads,
And thrown them away in the yard.

The Hen would have pranked up her feathers,
But plucking had sadly deformed her;
And for want of them she would have shivered with cold,
If the roasting she had had not warmed her.

And the Cock felt exceedingly queer:
He thought it a very odd thing

That his head and his voice were he did not know
where,
And his gizzard tucked under his wing.

The gizzard got into its place, —
But how, Santiago knows best;
And so, by the help of the Saint,
Did the liver and all the rest.

The heads saw their way to the bodies:
In they came from the yard, without check;
And each took its own proper station,
To the very great joy of the neck.

And in flew the feathers, like snow in a shower,
For they all became white on the way;
And the Cock and the Hen in a trice were refledged,
And then who so happy as they?

"Cluck! cluck!" cried the Hen right merrily then;
The Cock his clarion blew;
Full glad was he to hear again
His own cock-a-doo-del-doo!

PART III.

"A MIRACLE! a miracle!"
The people shouted, as they might well,
When the news went through the town;

And every child and woman and man
Took up the cry, and away they ran
To see Pierre taken down.

They made a famous procession:
My good little women and men,
Such a sight was never seen before,
And I think will never again.

Santiago's Image, large as life,
Went first, with banners and drum and fife;
And next, as was most meet,
The twice-born Cock and Hen were borne
Along the thronging street.

Perched on a cross-pole hoisted high,
They were raised in sight of the crowd;
And, when the people set up a cry,
The Hen she clucked in sympathy,
And the Cock he crowed aloud.

And because they very well knew for why
They were carried in such solemnity,
And saw the Saint and his banners before 'em,
They behaved with the greatest propriety
And most correct decorum.

The Knife, which had cut off their heads that morn,
Still red with their innocent blood, was borne, —
The scullion-boy he carried it;

And the Skewers also made a part of the show,
With which they were trussed for the spit.

The Cook in triumph bore that Spit
As high as he was able;
And the Dish was displayed, wherein they were laid
When they had been served at table.

With eager faith the crowd pressed round:
There was a scramble of women and men
For who should dip a finger-tip
In the blessèd Gravy then.

Next went the Alcade, beating his breast,
Crying aloud like a man distressed,
And amazed at the loss of his dinner, —
"Santiago, Santiago!
Have mercy on me, a sinner!"

And, lifting oftentimes his hands
Towards the Cock and Hen,
"*Orate pro nobis!*" devoutly he cried;
And as devoutly the people replied,
Whenever he said it, "Amen!"

The Father and Mother were last in the train:
Rejoicingly they came,
And extolled, with tears of gratitude,
Santiago's glorious name.

So, with all honors that might be,
They gently unhanged Pierre:
No hurt or harm had he sustained;
But, to make the wonder clear,
A deep, black halter-mark remained
Just under his left ear.

PART IV.

And now, my little listening dears,
With open mouths and open ears,
Like a rhymer whose only art is
That of telling a plain, unvarnished tale,
To let you know, I must not fail,
What became of all the parties.

Pierre went on to Compostella
To finish his pilgrimage:
His parents went back with him joyfully,
After which they returned to their own country;
And there, I believe, that all the three
Lived to a good old age.

For the gallows on which Pierre
So happily had swung,
It was resolved that never more
On it should man be hung.

To the Church it was transplanted,
As ancient books declare;
And the people in commotion,
With an uproar of devotion,
Set it up for a relic there.

What became of the halter I know not,
Because the old books show not;
But we may suppose and hope
That the city presented Pierre
With that interesting rope.

For in his family — and this
The Corporation knew —
It rightly would be valued more
Than any *cordon bleu.*

The Innkeepers' wicked daughter
Confessed what she had done:
So they put her in a convent,
And she was made a Nun.

The Alcade had been so frightened,
That he never ate fowls again;
And he always pulled off his hat
When he saw a Cock and Hen.

Wherever he sat at table,
Not an egg might there be placed;
And he never even mustered courage for a custard,

Though garlic tempted him to taste
Of an omelet now and then.

But always, after such a transgression,
He hastened away to make confession;
And not till he had confessed,
And the Priest had absolved him, did he feel
His conscience and stomach at rest.

The twice-born Birds, to the Pilgrim's Church,
As by miracle consecrated,
Were given; and there unto the Saint
They were publicly dedicated.

At their dedication, the Corporation
A fund for their keep supplied;
And, after following the Saint and his banners,
This Cock and Hen were so changed in their manners
That the Priests were edified.

Gentle as any turtle-dove,
Saint Cock became all meekness and love;
Most dutiful of wives,
Saint Hen she never pecked again:
So they led happy lives.

The ways of ordinary fowls,
You must know, they had clean forsaken;
And if every Cock and Hen in Spain
Had their example taken,

Why, then — the Spaniards would have had
No eggs to eat with bacon.

These blessèd Fowls, at seven years' end,
In the odor of sanctity died:
They were carefully plucked; and then
They were buried, side by side.

And, lest the fact should be forgotten,
(Which would have been a pity,)
'Twas decreed, in honor of their worth,
That a Cock and Hen should be borne thenceforth
In the arms of that ancient City.

Two eggs Saint Hen had laid, — no more;
The chicken were her delight:
A Cock and Hen they proved;
And both, like their parents, were virtuous and white.

The last act of the Holy Hen
Was to rear this precious brood; and, when
Saint Cock and she were dead,
This couple, as the lawful heirs,
Succeeded in their stead.

They also lived seven years;
And they laid eggs but two,
From which two milk-white chicken
To Cock and Henhood grew;

And always their posterity
The self-same course pursue.

Not one of these eggs ever addled,
(With wonder be it spoken!)
Not one of them ever was lost,
Not one of them ever was broken.

Sacred they are, — neither magpie nor rat,
Snake, weasel, nor marten, approaching them;
And woe to the irreverent wretch
Who should even dream of poaching them!

Thus, then, is this great miracle
Continued to this day;
And to their Church all Pilgrims go,
When they are on the way;
And some of the feathers are given them,
For which they always pay.

No price is set upon them,
And this leaves all persons at ease:
The Poor give as much as they can;
The Rich, as much as they please.

But that the more they give the better,
Is very well understood;
Seeing whatever is thus disposed of
Is for their own souls' good; —

For Santiago will always
Befriend his true believers ;
And the money is for him, the Priests
Being only his receivers.

To make the miracle the more,
Of these feathers there is always store,
And all are genuine too ;
All of the original Cock and Hen,
Which the Priests will swear is true.

Thousands a thousand times told have bought them ;
And, if myriads and tens of myriads sought them,
They would still find some to buy ;
For, however great were the demand,
So great would be the supply.

And if any of you, my small friends,
Should visit those parts, I dare say
You will bring away some of the feathers,
And think of Old Robin Gray.

NOTES TO THE PILGRIM TO COMPOSTELLA.

A ship, of marble made. — Introd. p. 201.

The marble ship I have not found anywhere, except in Geddes, who must have found it in some version of the legend which has not fallen into my hands. But that the ship was made of marble, I believe to be quite as true as any other part of the legend of Santiago. Whether of marble or not, it was a miraculous ship, which, without oars or sails, performed the voyage from Joppa to Iria Flava, now El Padron, in Galicia, in seven days.

Classical fables were still so passable when the "Historia Compostelana" was written, that the safe passage of this ship over the Syrtes, and between Scylla and Charybdis, is ascribed to the presiding hand of Providence. — *España Sagrada*, t. xx. p. 6.

His headless corpse. — Introd. p. 201.

How the body came to leave its head behind is a circumstance which has not been accounted for; and yet it requires explanation, because we are assured that Santiago took particular care not to part with his head when it was cut off.

"At the moment," says the annalist of Galicia, "when the cruel executioner severed from its neck the precious head of the sacred apostle, the body miraculously raised its hands and caught it, and in that posture it continued till night. The astonished Jews attempted to separate it, but in vain; for, upon touching the venerable corpse, their arms became cold, as if frozen, and they remained without the use of them." — *Añales de Galicia, por El Doctor D. Francisco Xavier Manuel de la Huerta y Vega.* Santiago, 1733.

"Cortada la cabeza no Dio en tierra,
Que por virtud de Dios, el con las manos,
Antes que cayga al suelo á si la afierra,
Que no pueden quitarsela tyranos."
Christoval de Mesa: El Patron de España, f. 62.

Perhaps his companions dropped it on their way to the coast; for the poet tells us they travelled in the dark, and in a hurry.

"Cubiertos de la noche con el manto
Sin que ningun contrario los impida,
Mas presto que si fueran á galope,
Llevan el cuerpo á la ciudad de Jope."
Ib. f. 65.

But, according to the "Historia Compostelana" (España Sagrada, t. xx. p. 6), there is the testimony of Pope St. Leo, that the original head came with the body.

And how, though then he had no head,
He afterwards had two. — Introd. p. 201.

This is a small allowance, and must be understood with reference to the two most authentic ones in that part of the world, — that at Braga, and one of the two at Compostella.

It is a common thing for saints to be polycephalous; and Santiago is almost as great a pluralist in heads as St. John the Baptist has been made by the dealers in relics. There are some half-dozen heads, and almost as many whole bodies, ascribed to him, — all in good odor, all having worked miracles, and all, beyond a doubt, equally authentic.

And how he used to fight the Moors. — Introd. p. 202.

Most appropriately, therefore, according to P. Sautel, was he called Boanerges.

"Conspicitur media cataphractus in aere ductor,
Qui dedit in trepidam barbara castra fugam.
Tam cito tam validæ cur terga dedere phalanges?
Nimirum Tonitru Filius ista patrat."
Annus Sacer Poeticus, vol. ii. p. 32.

— "Siendo acá en España nuestro amparo y defensa en las

guerras, merecio con razon este nombre: pues mas feroz que trueno ni rayo espantaba, confundia y desbarataba los grandes exercitos de los Moros." — *Morales, Coronica Gen. de España*, l. ix. c. vii. § 4.

"Vitoria España, vitoria,
que tienes en tu defensa,
uno de los Doze Pares;
mas no de nacion Francesa.
Hijo es tuyo, y tantos mata,
que parece que su fuerza
excede á la de la muerte
quando mas furiosa y presta."
Ledesma, Conceptos Espirituales, p. 242.

The Spanish clergy had a powerful motive for propagating these fables; their *Privilegio de los votos* being one of the most gainful as well as most impudent forgeries that ever was committed.

An old hymn, which was formerly used in the service of his day, likens this apostle to — a lion's whelp!

"Electus hic apostolus,
Decorus et amabilis,
Velut leonis catulus
Vicit bella certaminis."
Divi Tutelares, 229.

"Thirty-eight visible appearances," says the Padre Maestro Fray Felipe de la Gandara, chronicler-general of the kingdom of Galicia, — "thirty-eight visible appearances, in as many different battles, aiding and favoring the Spaniards, are recounted by the very learned Don Miguel Erce Gimenez, in his most erudite and laborious work upon the 'Preaching of Santiago in Spain;' from which work, the *illustrissimus* Doctor Don Antonio Calderon has collected them in his book upon the excellences of this apostle. And I hold it for certain that his appearances have been many more; and that, in every victory which the Spaniards have achieved over their enemies, this their great captain has been present with his favor and intercession." — *Armas i Triunfos del Reino de Galicia*, p. 648.

The Chronista General proceeds to say that Galicia may be especially proud of its part in all these victories, the saint having publicly prided himself upon his connection with that kingdom; for, being asked in battle once, who and what he was (being a stranger), he replied, "I am a soldier, a kinsman of the eternal King, a citizen and inhabitant of Compostella, and my name is James." For this fact, the chronicler assures us that a book of manuscript sermons, preached in Paris three centuries before his time by a Franciscan friar, is sufficient authority: "*es valiente autoridad!*" — *Armas i Triunfos del Reino de Galicia*, p. 649.

Santiago there they call him. — Introd. p. 202.

"The true name of this saint," says Ambrosio de Morales, "was Jacobo (that is, according to the Spanish form), taken with little difference from that of the Patriarch Jacob. A greater is that which we Spaniards have made, corrupting the word little by little, till it has become the very different one which we now use. From Santo Jacobo we shortened it, as we commonly do with proper names, and said Santo Jaco. We clipped it again after this abbreviation, and, by taking away one letter and changing another, made it into Santiago. The alteration did not stop here; but, because Yago or Tiago by itself did not sound distinctly and well, we began to call it Diago, as may be seen in Spanish writings of two or three hundred years old. At last, having passed through all these mutations, we rested with Diego for the ordinary name, reserving that of Santiago when we speak of the saint." — *Coronica General de España*, l. ix. c. vii. § 2.

Florez pursues the corruption further: "Nombrandole por la voz Latina Jacobus Apostolus con abreviacion y vulgaridad Jacobo Apostolo, ó Giacomo Postolo, ó Jiac Apostol." — *España Sagrada*, t. xix. p. 71.

It has not been explained how *Jack* in this country was transferred from James to John.

The Prior Cayrasco de Figueroa assures us that St. James was a gentleman, his father Zebedee being —

"Varon de ilustre sangre y Galileo,
Puesto que usava el arte piscatoria,
Que entonces no era illicito, ni feo,
Ni aora en muchas partes menos gloria,
La gente principal tener oficio,
O por su menester, ó su exercicio."
Templo Militante, p. iii. p. 83.

Morales also takes some pains to establish this point. Zebedee, he assures us, "era hombre principal, señor de un navio, con que seguia la pesca;" and it is clear, he says, "como padre y hijos seguian este trato de la pesqueria honradamente, mas como señores que como oficiales!" — *Coronica Gen. de España*, l. ix. c. vii. § 3.

They've an Inquisition to maul him. — Introd. p. 202.

Under the dominion of that atrocious tribunal, Ambrosio de Morales might truly say, "No one will dare deny that the body of the glorious apostle is in the city which is named after him, and that it was brought thither, and afterwards discovered there by the great miracles," of which he proceeds to give an account. "People have been burnt for less," as a fellow at Leeds said the other day of a woman whom he suspected of bewitching him.

There is nothing of which the Spanish and Portuguese authors have boasted with greater complacency and pleasure than of the said Inquisition.

All, who in their mortal stage
Did not perform this pilgrimage,
Must make it when they were dead — Introd. p. 203.

Fray Luys de Escobar has this among the five hundred proverbs of his Litany: —

"El camino á la muerte
Es como el de Santiago.
Las quatrocientas," &c. f. 140.

It seems to allude to this superstition; meaning, that it is a journey which all must take. The particular part of the pilgrimage which must be performed, either in ghost or in person, is that of crawling through a hole in the rock at El Padron, which the apostle is said to have made with his staff. In allusion to this part of the pilgrimage, which is not deemed so indispensable at Compostella as at Padron, they have this proverb: "Quien va á Santiago, y non va á Padron, ó faz Romeria ó non." The pilgrim, indeed, must be incurious who would not extend his journey thither. A copious fountain, of the coldest and finest water which Morales tasted in Galicia, rises under the high altar, but on the outside of the church: the pilgrims drink of it, and wash in its waters, as the apostle is said to have done. They ascend the steps in the rock upon their knees, and finally perform the passage which must be made by all: "y cierto, considerado el sitio, y la hermosa vista que de alli hay á la ciudad, que estaba abaxo en lo llano, y á toda la ancha hoya llena de grandes arboledas y frescuras de mas de dos leguas en largo, lugar es aparejado para mucha contemplacion." — *Viage de Morales*, p. 174.

One of Pantagruel's "Questions Encylopédiques" is, "Utrum le noir Scorpion pourroit souffrir solution de continuité en sa substance, et par l'effusion de son sang obscurcir et embrunir la voye lactée, au grand intérest et dommage des Lifrelofres Jacobipetes." — *Rabelais*, t. ii. p. 417.

The scallop-shell. — Introd. p. 203.

"The escallops, being denominated by ancient authors the 'Shells of Gales,' or 'Galicia,' plainly apply to this pilgrimage in particular." — *Fosbrooke*, *British Monachism*, p. 423.

Fuller is therefore mistaken, when, speaking of the Dacres family (Church Hist. cent. xii. p. 42), who gave their arms *gules*, three scallop-shells argent, he says, "Which scallop-shells (I mean the nethermost of them, because most concave and capacious), smooth within, and artificially plated without, was oft-times cup and dish to the pilgrims in Palestine, and thereupon their arms often charged therewith."

The staff was bored and drilled for those
Who on a flute could play. — Introd. p. 204.

Sir John Hawkins says "that the pilgrims to St. James of

Compostella excavated a staff, or walking-stick, into a musical instrument, for recreation on their journey." — *History of Music*, vol. iv. p. 139, quoted in *Fosbrooke's British Monachism*, p. 469. Mr. Fosbrooke thinks that "this ascription of the invention of the Bourdon to these pilgrims in particular is very questionable." Sir John probably supposed, with Richelet, that the Bourdon was peculiar to these pilgrims, and therefore that they had invented it.

Mr. Fosbrooke more than doubts the etymon from a musical use. "The barbarous Greek Βορδονια," he observes, "signified a beast of burden, and the Bourdon was a staff of support. But the various meanings of the word, as given by Cotgrave, make out its history satisfactorily. *Bourdon*, a drone, or dorre-bee (Richelet says 'grosse mouche, ennemie des abeilles'); also the humming or buzzing of bees; also the drone of a bagpipe; also a pilgrim's staff; also a walking-staff, having a sword, &c., within it.

"It was doubtless applied to the use of pitching the note, or accompanying the songs with which pilgrims used to recreate themselves on their journeys, and supposed by Menestrier to be hymns and canticles." — *Fosbrooke*, p. 422.

In Germany, "walking-sticks that serve as tubes for pipes, with a compressing pump at one end to make a fire, and a machine at the other for impaling insects without destroying their beauty, are common." ("Hodgkins's Travels," vol. ii. p. 135.) I have seen a telescope and barometer in a walking-stick, if that name may be applied to a staff of copper.

The twice-born Cock and Hen. — III. p. 211.

There is another story of a bird among the miracles of Santiago: the poor subject of the miracle was not so fortunate as the Cock and Hen of the Alcade; but the story is true. It occurred in Italy; and the Spanish fable is not more characteristic of the fraudulent practices carried on in the Romish church, than the Italian story is of the pitiable superstition which such frauds fostered, and which was, and is to this day, encouraged by the dignitaries of that church.

At the request of St. Atto, Bishop of Pistoja, the Pistojans say that some relics, taken from Santiago's most precious head, were given to their church by the Archbishop of Compostella, Diego Gelmirez, a person well known in Spanish history. "Nullus umquam mortalium hoc donum impetrare posset," he affirmed, when he made the gift; and the historian of the translator adds, "Quod verè a Domino factum credimus et non dubitamus, sicut manifestis et apertis indiciis manifestè et apertè miracula declarabunt." There is a good collection of these miracles, but this of the bird is the most remarkable.

"In those days," says the writer, "another miracle, as pious as it is glorious, was wrought by the Lord, in the which he who worthily perpends it will perceive what may pertain to the edification of all those who visit the shrine of Santiago, and of all faithful Christians. About three weeks after the consecration of Santiago's altar, a certain girl of the country near Pistoja was plucking hemp in a garden, when she observed a pigeon flying through the air, which came near her, and alighted; upon which she put up a prayer to the Lord Santiago, saying, 'O Lord Santiago, if the things which are related of thee at Pistoja be true, and thou workest miracles, as the Pistojans affirm, give me this pigeon, that it may come into my hands!' Forthwith the pigeon rose from the spot where it had alighted, and, as if it were a tame bird, came to her; and she took it in her hands, and held it there as if it had been lifeless. What then did the girl do? She carried it home, showed it to her father, and to him and the rest of the family related in what manner it had come to her hands. Some of them said, 'Let us kill and eat it;' others said, 'Do not hurt it, but let it go.' So the girl opened her hand to see what it would do. The pigeon, finding itself at liberty, fled to the ground, and joined the poultry, which were then picking up their food; nor did it afterwards go from the house, but remained in their company, as if it belonged to them.

"All therefore regarding, with no common wonder, the remarkable tameness of this pigeon, which indeed was not a tame bird, but a wild one, they went to a priest in the adjacent city, and acquainted him with the circumstances. The priest, giving good counsel to the girl and her father, as he was bound to do, said, 'We will go together to our lord the bishop, on Sunday, and act as he may think proper to direct us in this matter.' Accordingly, on the Sunday they went to Pistoja, and presented the pigeon to the bishop, who, with his canons, was then devoutly celebrating Mass, in honor of Santiago, upon the holy altar which had been consecrated to his honor. The prelate, when he had listened to their story, took the bird, and placed it upon the wall of the chancel, which is round about the altar of Santiago; and there it remained three weeks, never departing from thence, excepting that sometimes, and that very seldom, it flew about the church, but always returned without delay to its own station, and there mildly, gently, harmlessly, and tamely continued; and rarely did it take food.

"But people from Lucca, and other strangers, plucked feathers from its neck, that they might carry them away for devotion, and, moreover, that they might exhibit them to those who had not seen the bird itself. From such injuries it never attempted to defend itself, though its neck was skinned by this plucking; and this the unthinking people continued to do, till at length the pigeon paid the debt of nature. And it was no wonder that it died; for how could any creature live that scarcely ever ate or slept? People came thither night and day from all parts, and one after another disturbed it; and every night vigils were kept there, the clergy and the people with loud voices singing praises to the Lord; and many lights were continually burning there. How, therefore, could it live, when it was never allowed to be at rest? The clergy and people, grieving at its death, as indeed it was a thing to be lamented, took counsel, and hung up the skin and feathers to be seen there by all comers.

"In such and so great a matter, what could be more gratifying, what more convenient, than this wonderful sign which the Almighty was pleased to give us? There is no need to relate any thing more concerning the aforesaid pigeon: it was seen there openly and publicly by all comers; so that not only the laity and clergy of that city, but many religious people from other parts, — abbots, friars, clergy, and laity, — are able to attest the truth. And I also add this my testimony as a true and faithful witness; for I saw the pigeon myself for a whole week, and actually touched it with my own hands."

There is a postscript to this story, as melancholy as the tale itself. The sick and the crippled and the lame had been brought to this church, in expectation of obtaining a miraculous cure by virtue of the new relics which had arrived. Among these was a poor woman in the last stage of disease, who had been brought upon her pallet into the church, and was laid in a corner, and left there; nor was it observed that this poor creature was *in articulo mortis*, till the pigeon flew to the place and alighted upon her, and so drew the attention of the people in the church to the dying woman, "quam quidem, prout credimus, nisi columba monstrasset, nemo morientem vidisset." They removed her out of the church just before she breathed her last; and in consequence of this miracle, as it was deemed, they gave her an honorable funeral. — *Acta Sanctorum*, Jul. t. vi. p. 64.

What became of the halter I know not,
Because the old books show not. —IV. p. 214.

"Antiguedad sagrada, el que se arriedra
De te, sera su verso falto y manco."

So Christoval de Mesa observes, when he proceeds to relate how the rude stone, upon which the disciples of Santiago laid his body when they landed with it in Spain, formed itself into a sepulchre of white marble. — *El Patron de España*, f. 68.

END OF VOL. VII.

www.ingramcontent.com/pod-product-compliance
Lightning Source LLC
LaVergne TN
LVHW050527100826
845148LV00002B/466

* 9 7 8 1 4 2 5 5 1 9 7 8 0 *